SURVIVAL MANUAL

Tools to Manage Anger and Stress

DR. PAUL HARDY

SURVIVAL MANUAL
Tools to Manage Anger and Stress
Dr. Paul Hardy
Copyright Paul Hardy, 2024
All rights reserved.

Printed in the United States of America.
Cover image from Pixabay.com
Design by Paul Hardy

No part of this publication may be reproduced, stored in a retrieval system, or transmitted in any form or by any means electronic, mechanical, photocopying, recording or otherwise without prior written permission.
All Scriptures are taken from the World English Bible from the public domain
unless otherwise noted.

The author may be contacted at the following address
Dr. Paul Hardy
Consultingink
3609 Van Buren Dr.
Virginia Beach, Virginia 23452
Printed in the Unites States of America

Cover design by Paul Hardy
Chart designs by Paul Hardy
Pictures, Photographs, and Illustrations
by Pixabay unless otherwise noted
https://pixabay.com/images
Copyright 2024 by Paul A. Hardy. All rights reserved in all media.

AMAZON ISBN: 9798340767974

CONTENTS

ONE
UNDERSTANDING ANGER 8

TWO
REASONS OR EXCUSES? 15

THREE
UNDERSTANDING MYSELF 22

FOUR
THE EMOTIONAL TANK ……………….. 32

FIVE
CALM – CONNECT THE DOTS 45

SIX
CALM - ASK THE RIGHT QUESTIONS 56

SEVEN
CALM – LISTEN TO PEOPLE 63

EIGHT
CALM – MOVE ON OR MOVE OUT ………. 71

CONCLUSION 81

PREFACE

THE STRUGGLE IS REAL!

We all struggle at times. It may be the fallout from some of our bad choices, mistakes, or bad habits. Our personal struggles may come from habits we learned in a previous relationship, or childhood experiences. These can eventually create a lifestyle filled with serious consequences.

A CONTINUING PROBLEM

According to a 2019 poll, 84% of those surveyed believe that Americans are angrier today compared to a generation ago. When asked about their own feelings, 42% of respondents said they were angrier in the past year than they had been further back in time. This surge in anger can have implications for health, as it is considered a health risk by experts. Dr. Anil Jain, vice president and chief health information officer at IBM Watson Health, emphasizes the importance of understanding and managing anger from a health perspective. (Anger Poll: 84% Say We're Madder Than A Generation Ago : Shots - Health News : NPR. June 26, 2019. Scott Hensley)

Interestingly, the poll also explored how anger relates to news consumption and social media usage. Here are some key findings:

> **News and Anger:** 29% of people reported being often angry when checking the news, while 42% said the news sometimes made them angry.
>
> **Social Media and Anger:** Only 7% of people aged 65 and above said they were often angry when using social media, in contrast to 18% of those under 35. 28% of Seniors reported no social media usage, compared to only 2% of younger individuals who abstained.

In this program, we will explore ways to break down barriers and help you open up about the causes of your anger, acknowledging the roots of any problematic choices, so you will no longer run from your feelings or refuse to share them with others. (American Psychological Association, 2017),

THE GOOD NEWS IS

YOU can break free from whatever your struggle might be.

In this book, you will find the lessons you need to live a life of freedom. Your angry outbursts will no longer have control over your life. People will no longer feel "unsafe" around you. You can bring **CALM** to your biggest emotional storm.

Together, we will:

- **Build a strategy** to understand the process of your anger and how to work with it.
- **Integrate a new system** to understand personal reactions to stressful situations.
- **Demonstrate the use of the anger wheel** and other tools for anger and stress management.
- **List a series of appropriate questions** to find the sources of your anger or stress.
- **Apply the "CALM" method** to prepare you to deal with anger in a new way.

I have been working with people with relationship issues for over 40 years. Often, someone is angry, and a problem needs to be solved. Using the techniques in this book, MANY marriages and other relationships have been calmed down and restored.

1
UNDERSTANDING ANGER

ONE
UNDERSTANDING ANGER
OUR OBJECTIVE

To recognize the importance finding comfortable ways to express ourselves.

What you will learn in this chapter:

- Discover what's behind your anger.
- Recognize where in your body you experience anger.
- Observe the process of anger and how it builds.
- How to express your emotions using the "Wheel of Emotions.
- The concepts of the "Hyper-alert" brain.

Your story, your situation.

Some of us have a hard time acknowledging anything about our current situation. Many people run from their feelings and refuse to share them with others. It can be awkward and may make a person feel vulnerable or even weak. It can be hard to open up, especially to strangers who may not understand or accept their issues. We can become concerned, and run from talking out of a fear of . . .

◊ **Embarrassment:** You may be afraid that sharing your story and situation will embarrass you because of certain details that might make you look bad.

◊ **Criticism:** It can be a real concern that people will criticize you for certain actions you have taken.

◊ **Exposure:** You may be concerned that sharing your story will expose you and make you vulnerable to other people.

◊ **Privacy:** You may feel that your private life is nobody's business. Many people have been taught to never "air their dirty laundry."

◊ **Other**

_____

This is the time and place to start talking about your situation in a private, safe environment.

"Seek to understand, then be understood." Steven Covey

"Speak when you are angry, and you will make the best speech you will ever regret." Ambrose Bierce

Describe a time you saw someone speak when angry and could never take it back.

_____

_____

_____

_____

"Telling people what's going on inside of you doesn't make you weak, rather it's a sign of great courage!" Dr. Paul

Why do you think some people might have a hard time sharing in a group setting?

_____

_____

_____

_____

Which of the fears listed hits closest to home with you?

_____

_____

_____

_____

MANAGING YOUR ANGER
BY DISCOVERING WHAT'S BEHIND IT

Let's use the chart below to identify what may be behind some of your reactions or angry responses. Both anger and stress are energetic balls that show up in your body as a reaction to a perceived threat or disagreement. This reactive energy will find its way into your head, your chest, and/or your stomach. So, if you ignore it long enough, it can take on a life of its own and create all kinds of problems in your body.

WHERE DO YOU SENSE ANGER AND STRESS?

Defining Anger: Anger is emotion + energy. It is:

- an emotional state.
- intense energy.
- Inspiring powerful, often aggressive, feelings and behaviors.
- The energy to fight and defend ourselves when we are attacked.

Then, it requires a conscious response.

- We choose to react spontaneously in a negative way in trying to even the playing field.
- We choose to process the situation objectively and deal with the problem towards a viable solution.

Where in your body to you most experience stress and anger?

Although troublesome and frustrating things happen in life, how we respond to them matters the most. It's not becoming angry that creates the problem. It is:

- What we do with it, and
- How long it lasts.

 Now, let's look at the sequence and process of an anger incident. How it starts and what directions it may take.

How is talking about your internal life and struggles a sign of strength rather than weakness?

_____
_____
_____
_____

What might you add to the definition of stress and anger?

_____
_____
_____
_____
_____

Why do you think some people might have a hard time sharing in a group setting like this one?

_____
_____
_____
_____
_____

Where do you tend to store internal energy like stress and anger?

___ my head
___ my chest
___ my gut

What are the long-term effects of keeping this energy locked inside your body?

_____
_____
_____

THE PROCESS OF ANGER

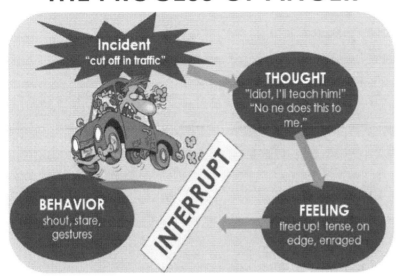

- **A TRIGGER, or INCIDENT: A person, or situation** happens. Someone says or does something, and you react or overreact to it. **This creates a ball of energy.**

- **INTERNAL REACTION: You have a response-thought.** You filter the event as either a positive or negative through your personal belief system.

    ◊**A Positive Response -** "Life happens." "People happen." "Maybe there's a bigger purpose in this." "There may be something I can learn from it."

    ◊**A Negative, Personalization Response,** "My life is awful." "I'm the worst person ever." "I'm never good enough." "Look what you made me do!" "You make my life awful." "You made me angry."

- **EMOTIONAL REACTION: Creates symptoms.** "Now, I feel bad. "I feel ashamed for being so angry." "I regret what I said and how I acted." "I'm a terrible person."

- **PHYSICAL REACTION: Creates symptoms.** Your body reacts "in kind" with the energy presented: sweaty palms, racing heart, clenched fists, and/or high blood pressure.

- **DECISION, CHOICE:** Either you do what comes naturally, and suffer the consequences, or you choose to **intentionally interrupt the pattern.**

- **EXTERNAL REACTIONS become behaviors and habits.** Either you release the energy and deal with it, or a fight ensues. The event either subsides or escalates. Worse things happen and there may be emotional, physical, or even legal consequences.

"There's a reason why we were born with two ears and one mouth!"

What can we do to avoid becoming angry?

- _____
- _____
- _____

Describe anything you would add to the "Process of Anger."

_____
_____
_____
_____
_____

Explain a belief system you might adopt to create positive responses as internal reactions to anger and stress.

_____
_____
_____
_____
_____

Share a habit that has been produced by prolonged internal anger or stress.

_____
_____
_____
_____
_____

EXPRESSING YOUR ANGER

Managing Your Anger Poster | CreativeTherapyStore.com

You can use this anger wheel as a bridge to share your emotions. Point to the emotion that you are experiencing and explain the why and how you are going through it.

Facts to Figure:

- *"You do not 'make me' feel anything I don't already feel."*
- *"You are not the source of my anger."*
- *"You are not my enemy."*
- *"Every angry episode / event is an opportunity for my growth."*

Troubling emotions that hide behind our anger. (circle the ones you struggle with most often)

◊ *Sadness*
◊ *Fear*
◊ *Frustration*
◊ *Guilt*
◊ *Disappointment*
◊ *Worry*
◊ *Embarrassment*
◊ *Jealousy*
◊ *Hurt*
◊ *Anxiety*
◊ *Shame*
◊ *Other*

RECOGNIZING EMOTIONS

Circle any words from the wheel that most often apply to you.

SURPRISED   SAD/DISCOURAGED   SCARED/AFRAID

HAPPY   PROUD   DISGUSTED

EMBARRASSED/ASHAMED   LONELY   MAD/ANGRY

NERVOUS/ANXIOUS   Other _____

 If anger is emotion + energy, then the instinctive, natural way to express it is to respond aggressively. Something must happen with the energy to change this.

"A State of Hyper – Alert"

People with anger issues sometimes live much of their lives in a state of "hyper-alert;" that is, always expecting the next crisis or critical incident to happen. This may create a constant seeking of ways to protect themselves, or others, from real or perceived threats.

At certain times, hypervigilance — staying highly alert — is useful. But when it happens all too often, you may start to feel depleted. Tense muscles. Room scan. A feeling that something "bad" is about to happen and you're unable to relax in your environment.

Living with hypervigilance can not only make it difficult to enjoy the present moment, but it can also take away from your relationships, work, school, and overall quality of life.

 Think of hypervigilance like a guard dog working overtime. Sometimes, the guard dog barks at intruders, and rightfully so. But other times, the guard dog barks at things that don't pose a direct threat, like leaves blowing into the yard or a mailman two blocks away.

As you can imagine, when the guard dog in your brain is on high alert at all times, it can drain your mental, physical, and emotional faculties. In a word, it's exhausting. But you can train the guard dog. (psychcentral.com)

Which word or words from the list stands out to you most? Why?

_____
_____
_____
_____

Think about why you might want help with anger management and answer the following questions with as much detail as possible.

"I became angry, (created an anger situation, or reacted with anger) because it seemed . . ."

_____
_____
_____
_____
_____

Describe anything around the situation which made it worse or contributed to it.

_____
_____
_____
_____

What is your inner guard dog like? When is he/she most agitated?

_____
_____
_____
_____

"HYPER-ALERT" DESCRIPTIONS
(Check the boxers of any that apply)

You sense that you/your:

- ☐ mind seems overly active. can't stop thinking and analyzing, won't shut off no matter what you do.
- ☐ body is wound up with nervous energy.
- ☐ senses are hyper-alert and overly sensitized, including any and all senses.
- ☐ feel jittery due to so much energy.
- ☐ have aches and pains because the body is so geared up.
- ☐ have trouble sitting still, resting, or sleeping because the body is so geared up with energy. have restless legs
- ☐ get frequent headaches, including migraines from the constant stimulation and alertness.
- ☐ stomach is nervous, queasy, or upset (digestive system), including gas pains, cramps, and diarrhea because of the constant energy.
- ☐ feel lightheaded, dizzy, and unsteady from the high alert feeling.
- ☐ get body jolts, tremors, and brain zaps.
- ☐ have muscle stiffness, tightness, tension, and pain. hot or cold flashes.
- ☐ sharp, shooting pains.
- ☐ mind and body always feel keyed up.

(Adapted from anxietycentre.com)

The key to resolving issues with the hyper-alert brain is to find peace and calm from the inner storm of the heart and mind. Peace can become a learned, consistent state of mind. We will look at this later in the book.

Master these concepts to move forward.

- **RECOGNIZE:** Recognize **where** you experience the angry energy in your body.
- **PROCESS:** How the process and sequence of anger most often plays out for you.
- **TALK:** Use the "Wheel of Emotions" as a bridge to discuss your experiences.
- **CALM:** Calm down when you feel "hyper-alert."

Since we have defined anger and stress as energy, let's go deeper into how we process it and even make excuses for our reactions.

Which of the hyper-alert symptoms best fits you when caught in an angering, anxiety-producing, or stressful situation?
Description:

_____
_____
_____
_____

Why I react this way:

_____
_____
_____
_____

What may have caused your brain to go into a state of "hyper-alert?"

_____
_____
_____
_____
_____

Which concept (s) do you believe you have now mastered from this chapter?

_____
_____
_____
_____
_____

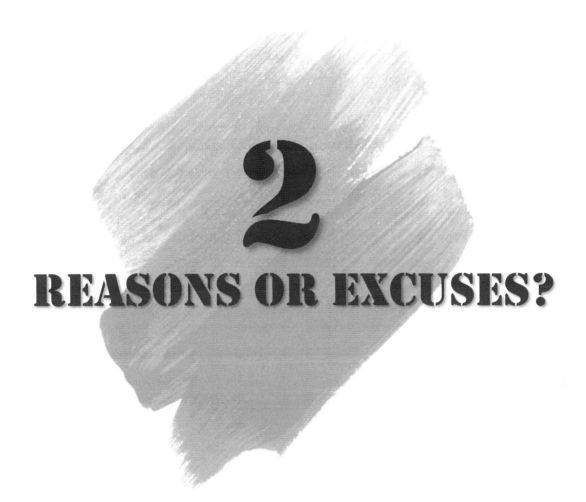

2
REASONS OR EXCUSES?

TWO
REASONS OR EXCUSES?

OUR OBJECTIVE

To explore any patterns or historic reasons for angry responses.

What you will learn in this chapter:

- Several reasons why people become angry.
- Compare constant anger to addiction.
- Recognize anger as an addiction in your life.

Matt's Story

Matt is a first responder. He has been in some very dangerous, life-threatening situations. He was sent to counseling because his superiors said he had a terrible attitude and was "edgy." He got into arguments with his co-workers and had a confrontation which didn't end well.

His specific job required him to be the first one on the scene quite often. He shares: "I had to shoot someone, but that wasn't the worst of it. This last time, it instantly reminded me of when I was in Afghanistan. I was a sniper . . . One of our guys had loaded the wrong ammo in our hummer and I watched at a distance as our guys were almost killed because they couldn't fight back. I wanted to kill that kid and I almost did, I choked him until he blacked out."

"Yeah, you could say I have an edge, but you have to, or something really bad could happen."

Matt must to come to understand:

- That was then and now is now.
- He was angry, with reason, because someone made a serious mistake.
- He does not have to be on edge at all times, this is not healthy or sustainable.
- He has unresolved anger from his battleground experience.
- He survived the previous experiences and can use those to build on current issues.

Anger is never without a reason, but seldom a good one. — Benjamin Franklin

Anger is a feeling that makes your mouth work faster than your mind.
Ritu Ghatourey

What question would you like to ask Matt about his story and situation?

_____
_____
_____
_____

What are some advantages to having self-discipline when it comes to anger?

_____
_____
_____
_____

"We look into our past, never to excuse ours, or someone else's behavior, but always to understand it." Dr. Paul

What should Matt do about "the edge" he has?

_____
_____
_____
_____

How could understanding your past help you get a grip with your anger?

_____
_____
_____
_____

FEELING THREATENED?

The hyper-alert brain can think it's being threatened by many things. It may always be on the watch. Others may view this as defensiveness, but it may very well be an attempt to protect something that is unseen. The internal parts of anger may be buried deep down inside us.

Think of it like this.

If we were all like chocolate-covered candies, the hard-colored outer shell would represent our anger and defensiveness. The chocolate on the inside would supposedly be protected by the hard-shell candy coating. (it never works, by the way, they melt in your hand if you hold them long enough).

(Circle any ways you tend to protect your heart)

HARSH WORDS   SARCASM   RAGE
LOUDNESS   INTELLECTUALIZING   DEFENSIVENESS
DEFLECTION   HUMOR   GASLIGHTING
RATIONALIZING   BLAME-SHIFTING

OTHER _____

If someone, or some certain situation in the present constantly "triggers" you into an angry response or episode, it most likely has some historic root in your life.

Let's say George is constantly belittling and putting his wife down with painful jabs and even punishments. He believes "she makes him so angry" much of the time. Later, we discover that George was bullied in school because he:
- had to wear glasses,
- wasn't good at sports,
- was overweight,
- was a nerd,
- was effeminate.

It is wise to direct your anger towards problems — not people; to focus your energies on answers — not excuses.
William Arthur Ward

Getting to Know You

When I get angry it's most often because...

_____
_____
_____

I became angry in the situation that brought me here because . . .

_____
_____
_____

The Candy Coating

My defensive, protective exterior "candy coating" tends to be . . . Because. . .

_____
_____
_____
_____

The people who originally tortured him are no longer available, so he bullies the people around him who are closest and mort vulnerable. George's wife is not the source, she is a trigger for some reason. George must learn to stop punishing her for what someone else did.

IF YOU'RE OFFEN ANGRY

Anger is a natural human emotion that can be triggered by various circumstances, events, and people that a person perceives as threatening, deceiving, frustrating, or disrespectful. It can also arise when people feel like their boundaries have been violated. Fear frequently lurks underneath the anger. Anger can point someone toward their unmet needs or may also indicate an obstacle that is blocking someone from reaching their goals.

There is no one reason why people are constantly angry. It's not that simple. Anger can be triggered from multiple angles. Here are a few categories:

☐ **PAIN: You may be hurting** - either physically or emotionally. You may avoid pain or may be trying to keep from being hurt again. It makes sense to avoid pain, but when a person is constantly dodging and running from even the hint of emotional pain, it Is not healthy. Some pain in life is even helpful because we learn and grow from it.

☐ **THREAT: You may feel frustrated** if things don't seem to be turning out the way you want them to. A threat to your expectations of life and people do not match the reality you must live with, it can be frustrating. Think about the following questions:

- Would an angry response change the situation, or solve the current problem?
- Is the problem situation worth being this upset over?
- How realistic is the specific expectation you have about this situation?

☐ **FEAR: You may be fearing something.** People are often afraid of being:
- Embarrassed, made fun of.
- Called out, publicly corrected or punished.
- Made to lose control of a situation.

Between pain, threat, and fear, which do you believe drives your anger more.

_____
_____
_____
_____

Can you ever see your angry response solving a current problem?

_____
_____
_____
_____
_____

If fear is a major motivator toward anger, when you feel threatened, ask yourself:

"What am I so afraid of, what is the worst that could happen?"

_____
_____
_____
_____
_____

This leads us to ask: **"Can Anger Be Addicting?"** Some people are constantly angry because they have become accustomed to acting this way. Anger and addictions have several things in common.

ANGER ADDICTION?

(check any boxes you agree with)

Let's think about it . . .

☐ **Both anger and addictions require us to admit there is a problem!** Substance use and addiction, as well as uncontrolled anger, can make our lives unmanageable. Until we recognize and admit this, nothing else gets better.

☐ **Both require us to be strong and** admit that we **need help**. Recovery is not for wimps, but for people who have the courage to work through their issues in life.

☐ **Both have a "snowball effect."** Life situations that have never been dealt with can just keep growing and growing and taking control of us. When anger responses are left unchecked, they create a large mass of energy that will find an outlet somewhere. Like a mega snowball at the bottom of the hill, we must deal with it before it grows.

☐ **Both require a process to be dealt with.** It is the process of learning and practicing new habits that will help us overcome anger management issues. Just as the process of recovery from substance use leads to a new, healthy life.

ANGER'S ALLURE
ARE YOU ADDICTED TO ANGER?

According to Psychology Today, there are reasons why anger can be a hard habit to break.

Anger is a public epidemic in America; it is involved in everything from media controversy to road rage to wars to mass shootings. But aside from the larger toxic scale of this basic human emotion and its connection to violence, anger affects us in our day-to-day personal lives as well, on an intimate scale. Everything from workplace frustration to family discord can erupt and contribute to overall stress, anxiety, and depression.

"Rather than deny or suppress our anger, what we really need to do is to learn to redirect it toward a workable solution."

Dr. Paul

How can approaching anger as an addiction change the way we deal with it?

_____
_____
_____
_____
_____

What are some "processes" you have seen work for other people?

_____
_____
_____
_____

Describe some recent anger or rage scenarios you've seen in the news:

_____
_____
_____
_____
_____
_____

BUT, WHY?

Why do we continue to bask in rage despite all the **dangerous consequences?** There can be legal, social, financial, physical, and medical ramifications. Here are some reasons why anger can be seen as an addiction:

☐ **Because the first step is admitting you have a problem.** For many, this is the hardest step until something happens that you can't take back. It takes maturity and guts to admit your anger has become a problem. Awareness is the first step to recovery (psychologytoday.com).

☐ **Your brain may enjoy being angry!** Part of the issue is that, in the moment, anger may feel good. It can override all other moral and rational brakes in the brain because it originates from our primordial, original limbic system (**survival instincts**): the brain center of our most automatic emotions like fear and desire.

☐ **Anger can bring on an emotional "rush."** Anger can lead to similar "rushes" like thrill-seeking activities. Danger triggers the dopamine reward receptors in the brain like other forms of addiction such as gambling, extreme sports, or even drugs like cocaine and methamphetamines. Anger can become its own reward, but like other addictions, the final consequences are dangerous and real.

☐ **Anger may point out a weakness in you.** Like it or not, we all have insecurities. The rush behind anger can be triggered by underlying feelings of weakness or insecurity, seeking to feel powerful in the moment and overcome those feelings. We call that, "compensating." We compensate for a weakness in many ways. We may think it helps us briefly feel like we're in control of things over which we typically have no control.

☐ **Anger may feel familiar and comfortable.** Unfortunately, for some people who are raised in continuously chaotic environments, the uncertainty and volatility of anger might become perversely comfortable. It can help distract from or escape underlying uncomfortable feelings of emptiness or fear. The rush of drama and conflict can feel familiar and produce a sense of intimacy that some might prefer rather than confront other darker emotions like loss or grief or more. Aside from traumatic family environments, combat veterans are also at risk of similar addiction, as they remain in high-threat situations for long and repeated periods of time.

How willing are you to take the FIRST step in admitting that anger has become a problem for you?

__ *Absolutely not*
__ *Not quite there yet*
__ *Somewhat willing*
__ *Very willing*

Describe any times your anger may have felt like a "rush" or pleasurable to you.

_____
_____
_____
_____

What are the top 3 consequences you've had from your anger?

1. _____
2. _____
3. _____

"Anger can be a kind of compensation that makes a person feel more in control because they feel so out of control."
Dr. Paul

Do you ever sense your anger might be a type of compensation because it makes you feel you are in control or successful?

_____
_____
_____
_____

Jim Folk of Anxiety Centre explains, "It has been estimated that 75 - 90 percent of all visits to primary care physicians are for stress related problems.

Job stress is far and away the leading source for adults but stress levels have also escalated in children, teenagers, college students, and the elderly for other reasons.

The Big Link

Stress and anger are two different emotions, but they are often linked. Stress is a response to a situation or event that is perceived as challenging or threatening. Sound familiar?

It can be caused by both positive and negative experiences, and it can show up in physical, emotional, and behavioral symptoms.

Anger, on the other hand, is an emotional state that is usually triggered by a perceived threat, injustice, or frustration. It is often accompanied by physiological changes such as increased heart rate, blood pressure, and muscle tension. Although stress and anger are different, they can be related. For example, chronic stress can lead to irritability and anger, while anger can cause stress and anxiety. Stress "is the wear and tear of everyday life."

As we all know, some days seem more stressful than others and some times it seems there is no letup. Daily stress is unavoidable and if it was properly managed, it wouldn't cause too many health problems. On-going stress, however, when not managed well, is at the root of a great many illnesses.

Master these concepts to move forward.

- **KNOW:** Know **why** you get angry.
- **NAME:** Give your angry emotion a name to deal with it better.
- **ADDICTION:** Treat your anger as an addiction.
- **AWARENESS:** Become aware of your stressors.

If anger is a protective outer candy-coating shell that can become seriously addicting, then we must recognize it as a problem and grow to understand ourselves better.

What kinds of stress come from your work situation?

_____
_____
_____

If stress is "the wear and tear of everyday life," list your top stressors.

1 _____
2 _____
3 _____
4 _____

Which concept (s) do you believe you have now mastered from this chapter?

_____
_____
_____
_____

3
UNDERSTANDING MYSELF

THREE
UNDERSTANDING MYSELF

OUR OBJECTIVE

Connect how your personality type interacts with appropriate expressions and actions.

What you will learn in this chapter:

- Compare aggression and anger management.
- How to use the 5-Minute Personality Test.
- Understanding different personalities and how they react to   anger.

Felipe's Story

Felipe is a fighter. He has fought and bullied his way through life. He is known as someone you wouldn't want to mess with. "I just have a rough personality, you know? I can't help it if I'm surrounded by stupid people who all seem to want to fight me."

A bar fight with several injuries landed him in trouble. Eventually, Felipe came to understand that it is not his personality, but his attitude and words that get him into trouble. When he realized that being abandoned by his father created a certain rage within him, he was able to let that go and become much calmer.

Felipe believes:

- "No one has the right to mess with me for any reason. I have to get the respect of everyone around me."
- "If you challenge me, I have to come back at you to prove I'm bigger and badder than you are."
- "I don't care about the consequences; you will not mess with me." (This behavior landed him in jail for assault charges).
- He must learn to pick his battles and not see "everything and everyone" as a threat.

Anger makes you smaller, while forgiveness forces you to grow beyond what you are.

Psychological fact:

"Anger is a natural defense against pain. When someone says 'I hate you,' they really mean, 'You hurt me'"

How would interpreting someone's anger toward you from "I hate you," to "You hurt me" change your attitude about it?

_____
_____
_____
_____

What questions would you like to ask Felipe?

_____
_____
_____

If Felipe doesn't change, how do you envision his future?

_____
_____
_____

WHAT IS AGGRESSION?

Aggression refers to a range of behaviors that can result in both physical and psychological harm to yourself, others, or objects in the environment.

It can be distinguished from anger in that anger is oriented at overcoming the target but not necessarily through harm or destruction. When such behavior is purposefully performed with the primary **goal of intentional injury or destruction**, it is termed hostile aggression.

Other types of aggression are less deliberately damaging and may be instrumentally motivated (proactive) or affectively motivated (reactive).

- Instrumental aggression involves an action carried out principally to achieve another goal, such as acquiring a desired resource.

- Affective aggression involves an emotional response that tends to be targeted toward the perceived source of the distress but may be displaced onto other people or objects if the disturbing agent cannot be attacked (see displaced aggression) (https://dictionary.apa.org/aggression)

Anger and its cousin, **aggression**, are often confused. **Anger** is an emotion you primarily feel inside. **Aggression** is behavior others can observe. So, you can be angry without being aggressive!

Aggressive behavior is typically shown against other people and includes actions like:

- Emotional punishment
- Throwing things
- Pushing, kicking, shoving
- Hitting
- Verbal bullying
- Scratching someone's car
- Hiding office supplies from a co-worker you dislike, etc.. (Tafrate and Kassinove, 2019)
- Other

When do you see aggression becoming "hostile aggression?"

_____
_____
_____
_____
_____

What do you think aggression most often does to its target?

_____
_____
_____

Anger tends to operate on the inside, aggression operates on the outside.

Describe any aggressive behaviors you struggle with:

_____
_____
_____

IT'S A THANG

Once we become aware that our angry responses are simply a **thing** to be dealt with (a problem to be solved), we can learn to deal with situations differently. Anger is a very individual thing, that is, what frustrates one person may have no meaning or reaction to another, and vice versa.

 Let's take a simple, 5-minute personality test to discover how we see ourselves. This can also help us gain more insight as to how others may see us.

Reframe your angry response as "a thing" to be dealt with, rather than an extension of yourself,

_____

_____

_____

_____

THE 5- MINUTE PERSONALITY TEST

	L / D	R / I	O / S	T / C
1	☐ I like to be in authority	☐ I'm excited about life!	☐ I can be emotionally sensitive	☐ I like to follow instructions
2	☐ I like to take charge	☐ I don't mind taking risks	☐ I tend to be a loyal person	☐ I want things to be accurate
3	☐ I am determined	☐ I tend to be a visionary	☐ People say I'm calm, even keeled	☐ I thrive on consistency, processes
4	☐ I'm enterprising, I need to be busy	☐ I'm very verbal, outspoken	☐ I enjoy my routines, they provide security	☐ I'm comfortable when things are predictable
5	☐ I tend to be very competitive	☐ I like to promote things	☐ I don't like change	☐ I'm a very practical person
6	☐ I like to solve problems	☐ I enjoy being popular, a people-person	☐ I give in to people easily	☐ I base my decisions on facts not emotions
7	☐ I have to be productive	☐ I'm fun-loving with people	☐ I avoid confrontation of any kind	☐ I'm a conscientious worker
8	☐ I tend to be a decision maker	☐ I like variety in my life	☐ I tend to be sympathetic with people	☐ I tend to be a perfectionist
9	☐ I'm bold about what I believe in	☐ I tend to be spontaneous	☐ I am a nurturing person	☐ I give a lot of attention to detail
10	☐ I can be very persistent	☐ I love to inspire people	☐ I tend to be a peacemaker	☐ I analyze things a lot
	__ TOTAL L	__ TOTAL R	__ TOTAL O	__ TOTAL T

EXPLAINING THE 4 PERSONALITIES

L - THE DIRECT – AGGRESSIVE. "Being direct with people is the only way to go. It seems I hurt people because I am most often 'brutally honest.' I don't even know I'm doing it most of the time. People just tell me I'm harsh and hurtful."

LIONS AND LIONESSES that Dominate tend to be Productivity oriented. If you want something done call on a lion or lioness. They are strongly oriented towards productivity and like to see forward movement to get things done. They tend to be very confident and self-reliant. They will take charge when necessary and enjoy it.

They make great coaches, entrepreneurs, directors, leaders, producers. This is why they constantly talk about what they "do" and ask the people around them what they are "up to or doing." They can be charging, hard driving, tireless extroverts.

(Dominant-Choleric) Other ways to describe Lions and Lionesses are "Tanks," "Mack Trucks," or "Grenade Launchers."

Weaknesses. They can be very blunt without considering people's emotions and tend to be impatient. They may not think through the processes or consequences of their hurried actions. Lions can even be mean, harsh, brash, hurtful, inconsiderate, and aggressive.

Deepest needs. Lions and lionesses really need to see improvements, forward movement, and new challenges. They need to feel that they are making a difference by solving problems in the world. If not, they become frustrated and may feel useless.

Anger meter. What makes lions angry is other people who are not effective or productive that might get in their way.

Interpersonal Conflicts. They can explode with anger. They may always seem to be on edge and extremely hard to please. They forge their way through life without considering the feelings of others, leaving hurt people in their wake. They have extremely high expectations.

Describe any other behaviors you have observed in "lion/lioness" types.

_____
_____
_____
_____

How do you usually deal with the lions/lionesses in your life?

_____
_____
_____
_____

How do lions/lionesses usually deal with their weaknesses?

_____
_____
_____
_____

What kinds of conflicts do you see lions/lionesses instigate?

_____
_____
_____
_____

What Works with Lions?

- Do your best to be cool, even distant with a calm response. This helps you maintain a level of control over the situation.
- Choose your battles carefully. Don't fight about everything, prioritize your battles.
- Set specific boundaries for arguments.
- In extreme cases, the only way to deal with a bully is to get a bigger bully. If they are dangerously aggressive, get help. Dr. Paul
- A soft answer turns away anger. DO NOT engage in their war, let them own it.
- Build them up as much as possible. Encourage them in their strengths. Lean in to help them pat themselves on the back. Compliment them and seek their advice.

A Simple Solution for the lion/lioness: Try putting yourself in the other person's place to sense what they feel with your attitudes, words, and actions. Treat others as you would wish to be treated.

What do you like most about lions/lionesses?

_____

_____

_____

R/I – INFLUENCERS. THE NUCLEAR REACTOR.
"I usually have an immediate and emotional response to most anything! I just can't hold it in, when I'm upset, I have to get it out."

RETRIEVERS that Influence tend to be People-oriented. This is the most exciting person in the group. They love to have fun and talk over everybody else. They enjoy motivating and inspiring other people and tend to be good at networking.

(Influencer-Sanguine) Other ways to describe the lab, "dreamer," "life of the party," They like to try impressing you, name-dropping and comparing.

Weaknesses. They can be unrealistic, disorganized, and give more credence to emotion than fact.

Deepest needs. Retrievers like to have social interaction and activities that are enjoyable without schedule or accountability.

Anger meter. What frustrates retrievers the most is when people do not consider their emotions and needs, and/or those of other people.

Describe any other behaviors you have observed in retrievers.

_____

_____

_____

How do you usually deal with the retrievers in your life?

_____

_____

_____

How do retrievers tend to deal with their weaknesses?

_____

_____

Interpersonal Conflicts. They are often controlled by their emotions and their emotions show all around them. They tend to be people-pleasers and people-focused. They are often the most boisterous, fun-loving, gregarious people in the crowd. You know they have arrived. They tend to brag and talk about themselves most often.

What Works with Retrievers?

- Get their attention, look them in the eye.
- Use touch to reach their heart.
- Express specific boundaries for behavior.
- Learn to go out with them in society.
- Accentuate their good qualities.

To connect with a retriever, you have to get them to envision and "feel" through their commitments. Dr. Paul

A Simple Solution for the retriever: Try slowing down and cooling your reactions down a bit. Take a step back and look at the bigger picture before you over react. .

O/S - THE STUFFER. AVOIDER / PASSIVE. "I carry a lot of inner anxiety. I worry a lot, but I pretend everything is fine on the outside. Then later, I'm angry and frustrated with myself and others. Since I don't usually react quickly, I tend to seethe, then lash out later."

OWLS that are Steady tend to be Philosophy oriented. If you're looking for someone who will be loyal and absorb the emotional pain of people around them, that's the owl. They are more observers than activists and make great listeners by sharing empathy. Owls want the world to be in harmony and work well together.

(Steady – Melancholic) Other ways to describe the Owl, "EEOR," "Debbie Downer," "Sniper," "Yes Person."

Weaknesses. Because owls are so in depth it can be very hard for them to make decisions as they try to seek every angle and possibility to decide. They can go into long discussions about philosophical ideas without realizing that others are not keeping up with them in the discussion. They can be overly critical, with a negative filter that taints everything they see around them. So, they complain and whine their way through life.

Describe a time you saw a retriever become angry:

_____
_____
_____

What conflicts have you seen retrievers get involved in?

_____
_____
_____
_____

How do you usually deal with the owls in your life?

_____
_____
_____
_____

Describe a philosophical conversation you've had with an owl:

_____
_____
_____

How have you seen owls deal with their weaknesses?

_____
_____
_____
_____

Deepest needs. Owls seek security at any cost. They need time to adjust to any kind of change and do their best in an environment that has no conflict.

Anger meter. They can become very angry and frustrated when people do not follow necessary proc-+*+esses and try to skip over important steps. They are also frustrated with any type of confrontation, but what really bothers them is if there is disunity or disharmony among a group.

Interpersonal Conflicts. Because owls tend to be observers, they may clash with people who constantly pressure them to get out more, or to become more involved beyond their level of comfortability.

What Works with Owls?

- Avoid deep or philosophical conversations with this person. They will last for hours with no conclusion.
- Don't let them blame you for something you didn't do.
- Try to help them see positive things in life. Point out good things.
- Do not pressure them to be around people unless you can help them see it as an advantage.
- Answer their long discussions with the minimal response.

Provide opportunities for introverts to engage with people or groups, but make sure it is their idea. Dr. Paul

A Simple Solution for the owl: Try taking baby steps like being open with someone you trust a little bit at a time. Test the idea of opening up and responding to someone without emotion. If it goes well, then you can try a little more.

T/C - TURTLES that are Cautious tend to be Process oriented.

If you want something done right going through the proper procedures, you're looking for a turtle. They love instruction manuals and are great at providing quality control. They thrive on consistency and routine. They have a strong need to maintain high standards in any situation.

(Calm – Phlegmatic) Are also known as "realists" and "bean counters."

How do owls tend to get their needs met?

What is your greatest struggle with owls?

How would you calm down a stressed owl?

Describe any other behaviors you have observed in turtle types.

What do you like most about turtles?

How do turtles tend to deal with their weaknesses?

Weaknesses. Because they are more observers than activists, they can be very critical of other people when things are not done perfectly to their standards. This makes them overly cautious. They can be passive-aggressive, unemotional, isolated, stoic, and can be hard to read.

Deepest needs. Turtles seek time alone and need to have as much security as possible to think through their own processes.

Anger meter. Turtles do not like to be rushed and become angry when they are forced to be around people when they need time alone.

Interpersonal Conflicts. They hide their emotions and spend much of their time inside the turtle shell. Anxious and depressed, they may find it hard to come out into the real world, so they hide in depression, inwardly angry and frustrated. They may keep lists of grievances taped to the inside of the shell. Codependent, they can easily let others make their decisions.

What Works with Turtles?

- Learn to speak their language even if they only use grunts or gestures.
- Get involved in his/her world as much as they will let you.
- Give them limited time for cave time (hibernation).
- Present ideas, without expecting an immediate response.
- Don't assume their silence is just about you. Dr. Paul

A Simple Solution for the turtle: Take a few minutes to speed up some things in your life. Take out one of your lists of imperfections and find speedy solutions for several of them.

Most of us have 2 dominant personality characteristics.
One may be higher than the other. The combination helps us understand our natural patterns and reactions and also identify areas to work on.

Master these concepts to move forward.

- **REPLACEMENT:** Avoid aggressive behaviors and replace them with kind assertiveness.
- **PERSONALITY:** Learn to work with your strengths and develop your weaker areas by comparing them to the 4 personality styles.
- **STRENGTHS:** Apply these principles to working with others in their strengths and weaknesses.

What is your greatest personal struggle with turtles?

_____
_____
_____
_____

Describe what type of personality comes out when it comes to anger:

_____
_____
_____
_____

Explain how describing our personalities can help us with anger management.

_____
_____
_____
_____
_____

➡ We have looked at the definition of aggression and discovered your specific personality type. This will help you understand your strengths and weaknesses regarding anger management.

The following chart will help you see the interactions of the different personality types. People may interact with any of these types in a given situation if a change in theor personality is required. But, the tendency is to return to home base.

If an opposite, or counter action is required of someone long-term, it will become stressful and frustrating for the person.

Direct Hot Spots
LOOK OUT FOR: Boredom, Relieving Stress with Substances
SOLUTIONS: Exercise, Set smaller goals

Influencer Hot Spots
LOOK OUT FOR: Feeling Disconnected from People, Loneliness
SOLUTIONS: Go to Small Meetings

ACTIVE EXTROVERTS

Direct
TENDS TO BE: PRODUCTIVE
Direct, Determined, Goal & Success-Oriented
Rushed, Competes & Controls, Builds
NEEDS TO DEVELOP:
Sharing Control, Delegating

Influencer
TENDS TO BE: PEOPLE PERSON
Self-Expressive, Influential
Charismatic, Emotionally Sensitive
NEEDS TO DEVELOP:
Discipline, Completing Tasks

TASK-ORIENTED — **PEOPLE-ORIENTED**

Cautious
TENDS TO BE: PENSATIVE
Analyzes Information, Creates
Faithful, Details, Sensitive, Avoids Risks
NEEDS TO DEVELOP:
Positive Outlook, Big Picture View

Stable
TENDS TO BE: PROCESSOR
Calm Under Pressure, Resists Change,
Routine, Compassionate, Caring, Careful
NEEDS TO DEVELOP:
Leadership, More Action

PASSIVE INTROVERTS

Cautious Hot Spots
LOOK OUT FOR: Worry, Overthinking, Using substances out of Fear
SOLUTIONS: Have Faith, Be Positive

Stable Hot Spots
LOOK OUT FOR: Lack of Decision and Action, Using out of Hopelessness
SOLUTIONS: Keep Active Help Others

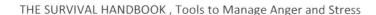

4
THE EMOTIONAL TANK

FOUR
THE EMOTIONAL TANK
OBJECTIVE

Envision the people around us as "love tanks" that need to be filled.

What you will learn in this chapter:

- Ways to detect and fill the emotional tanks of the people around you.
- A review the sequence of anger triggers.
- Concepts to deal with the heart of the matter in anger management.

Daria and James Story

Daria keeps asking James to listen to her. She feels ignored. She feels he does not care about her needs and is, in her words, "a selfish beast." "All he cares about is himself and all he wants from me is sex." She shares that she has tried everything, nagging, ignoring his existence, etc. Daria feels like she is running on empty and has nothing left to give James.

When asked what she wants from the relationship, she responds, "I don't know, but it's for sure not this. Every time we argue, he changes the topic, so I have to remind him of all the times he's forgotten or failed to meet my needs. I just don't know if I want to be in this relationship anymore!"

Daria and James:

- James needs to realize that Daria has needs he does not meet, and this makes her vulnerable and angry.
- Daria must get James' attention in positive ways and learn to reinforce any positive behaviors.
- Daria needs to define what her needs are, then share those specific needs in behavioral, specific, and relatable ways so James can see when he gets things right with her.
- If she started with a clear and concise statement of what she wants to say, this could help James understand the main idea of her message..
- James needs to focus on the issue at hand and avoid unrelated chatter or dredging up the past. This will help them both stay engaged and focused.

"Anybody can become angry – that is easy, but to be angry with the right person and to the right degree and at the right time and for the right purpose, and in the right way – that is not within everybody's power and is not easy."
– Aristotle

How can you know when you should be angry with someone?

_____
_____
_____

What could Daria and James do differently to resolve their issues?

_____
_____
_____

What would you like to ask them if you could?

_____
_____
_____

FILLING THE EMOTIONAL TANK

If we could envision each person around us as an emotional bank, a "love tank," it might help us learn to better meet their needs. Everyone has emotional needs, some more than others. Every day, we get to make deposits into their tank, or we subconsciously, or on purpose, make withdrawals. The more withdrawals we

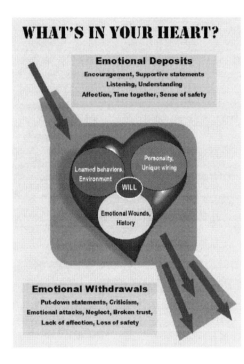

Realize that people's needs are important. We all have physical, emotional, and even spiritual needs. When these are not met, people around us may become frustrated. So, it's important to help meet these needs.

It's like this. Everyone has an emotional tank. Every day when the person wakes up, it's on empty.

Now, if you make emotional deposits into that person's emotional tank, they should feel appreciated and valued. But, if you make withdrawals from an empty tank, what do you get? A deficit, and eventually could end up in bankruptcy!

Our positive words of support, recognition, affection, and time with the person make deposits. Most often, these will make a person feel valued and respected. But a critical word, or snarky remark, our absence, or can empty it quickly. https://ousoescrever.com/2019/07/19/when-her-emotional-tank-is-empty/

➡ We have looked at the definition of aggression and discovered your specific personality type. This will help you understand your strengths and weaknesses regarding anger management. Now, let's look at more of the characteristics that may describe us as "an angry" person.

When you think of people as "emotional, love tanks," what deposits do you enjoy making to help fill them up?

_____
_____
_____

What types of withdrawals do you now want to avoid making?

_____
_____
_____
_____

Hatred stirs up strife, but love covers all offenses. Proverbs 10:12

How can ignoring an offense effect a person's love tank?

_____
_____
_____

If you make withdrawals from an empty tank, what do you eventually get?

_____
_____
_____

What can you do this week to make the people around you feel valued and respected?

_____
_____
_____

How can you deal with someone who has insatiable emotional needs when it seems their "love tank" is never full?

_____
_____
_____
_____

THE MILLER-PATTON ANGER SELF-ASSESSMENT

Put a check mark by any statements might describe you.

- [ ] I use abusive language, name-calling, insults, sarcasm or swearing.
- [ ] People tell me I become too angry, too quickly.
- [ ] I am easily annoyed and irritated and then it takes a long time to calm down.
- [ ] When I think about the bad things people did to me, or the unfair deals that I have gotten in life, I still get angry.
- [ ] I often make critical, judgmental comments to others, even if they do not ask for my advice or help.
- [ ] I use passive-aggressive behaviors, such as ignoring the other person or promising to do something and then "forgetting" about it to get the other person to leave me alone.
- [ ] At times, I use aggressive body language and facial expressions, like clenching my fists, staring at someone, or deliberately looking intimidating.
- [ ] When someone does or says something that angers me, I spend a lot of time thinking about what cutting replies I should have used at the time or how I can get revenge.
- [ ] I use self-destructive behaviors to calm down after an angry outburst such as drinking alcohol or using drugs, gambling, eating too much and vomiting, or cutting myself.
- [ ] When I get really angry about something, I sometimes feel physically sick (headaches, nausea, vomiting, diarrhea, etc.) after the incident.
- [ ] It is very hard to forgive someone who has hurt me even when they have apologized and seem very sorry for having hurt me.
- [ ] I always have to win an argument and prove that I am "right."
- [ ] I usually make excuses for my behavior and blame other people or circumstances for my anger (like job stress, financial problems, etc.).
- [ ] I react to frustration so badly that I cannot stop thinking about it or I can't sleep at night because I think about things that have made me angry.
- [ ] After arguing with someone, I often hate myself for losing my temper.
- [ ] Sometimes I feel so angry that I've thought about killing another person or killing myself.
- [ ] I get so angry that sometimes I forget what I said or did.
- [ ] I know that some people are afraid of me when I get angry, or they will "walk on eggshells" to avoid getting me upset.
- [ ] At times I have gotten so angry that I have slammed doors, thrown things, broken items, or punched walls.
- [ ] I have been inappropriately jealous and possessive of my partner, accusing him or her of cheating even when there was no evidence that my partner was being unfaithful.
- [ ] Sometimes I have forced my partner to do sexual behavior that he or she does not want to do, or I have threatened to cheat on my partner if he/she does not do what I want them to do to please me sexually.
- [ ] At times I have ignored my partner on purpose to hurt him or her but have been overly nice to other family members or friends.
- [ ] I have kept my partner dependent on me or socially isolated so that I can control and manipulate their feelings and actions so they will not leave me or end our relationship.
- [ ] I have used threats to get my way or win an argument.

SCORING THE MILLER-PATTON

Note: This test is an informal screening test to help you find out more information about your own feelings and expressions of anger. It is not intended to be a formal assessment.

- [ ] If you checked **10 or more** of these questions, you most likely have moderate-to-severe anger problems.
- [ ] If you checked **5 questions**, you are most likely at risk for having a problem with your anger.
- [ ] Even if checked **just one** of the questions, it may be helpful to learn some anger management techniques to improve your coping skills.
- [ ] If you checked "Sometimes I feel so angry that I've thought about killing another person or killing myself." please get immediate help, call 911. (betterdaysandnights.com)

THE KEY TO ANGER MANAGEMENT

Learn to Connect the Dots through Problem-Solving.

This is the key to longevity in relationships. "How can we solve this problem together?"

Now, let's look at the process and sequence of an angry episode again to process other thoughts, feelings, and actions.

A TRIGGER HAPPENS

Let's say, out of nowhere, an event, person, or situation presents itself. Someone says something, or there is an incident you cannot control. You have to make a decision. What will you do, fight back at it, or flight away from it.

This triggers a thought pattern. There is a discussion in your head that begins to create a plan. You may be very imaginative about what you might do, what you, could do, and what you would do.

THEN, THE RESPONSES/REACTIONS BEGIN

This sends a stress signal to your brain. You feel you have to do something. Fight or flight. You ask yourself, "What's this doing inside my body?"

Did you find any surprises from taking the Miller-Patton assessment?

_____
_____
_____

Go back over the ones you recognize in yourself and think of solutions for them.

_____
_____
_____
_____
_____
_____
_____
_____

If the key to anger management is to work together with others toward problem-solving, What is the biggest problem you've needed to solve that has caused you so much anger?

_____
_____
_____

How can you team up with others to solve your problem?

_____
_____
_____

A CALL TO ACTION

Then, what will you do about it? You may become aggressive and lash out with harsh words or actions. If you do what comes naturally, this could create several problems that, in turn put numerous consequences into action. Something that starts out as a skirmish ends up being a war!

A personal example. You're standing around some friends. Someone you don't know well makes a stupid, snide comment about you. (I've seen this happen many times, by the way) You're trying to work on your anger management skills, so you don't react quickly, but you see yourself doing something you might both regret. Then you think, I'll settle this with him later and do something really sinister (passive-aggressive).

Fortunately for everyone, you choose to let it go, so you have time to process and calm your brain down. Then, you use the following chart. The beauty of the **TFA** chart is that you can be anywhere at any time and pull out a little piece of paper and create the chart to process the situation.

> *A soft answer turns away wrath, but a harsh word stirs up anger. Proverbs 15:1*
>
> *Share a recent personal example when a situation got out of control.*
>
> _____
>
> _____
>
> _____
>
> *Escalating is when two people engage in anger layer, after layer until it gets out of hand. Like climbing the steps of an escalator. How can your soft answer slow an escalating situation down?*
>
> _____
>
> _____
>
> _____

On the next page is a **"TFA Trigger Chart."** It's purpose is to help you recognize triggers on a regular basis. You can use your own paper, or you can even use a napkin in a hurry.

1. Describe a recent **trigger.** Someone said or did something that upset you. Something out of your control came up.
2. Write down your **thoughts** about the trigger. What did you think about the trigger, mentally, objectively.
3. Move on to your **responses** to the trigger. Describe your emotional reaction internally.
4. Then, process what your **actions**, or reactions were both positive and negative. What choices did you make?

This will help you learn to work through episodes with more forethought and control.

THE TFA TRIGGER CHART

Describe a RECENT TRIGGER   Date _____

TRIGGER THOUGHTS	FEELINGS/RESPONSES	ACTIONS
What's on my mind?	How do I react?	What will I do?
TRIGGER	EMOTIONAL REACTION	CHOICE
	EXAMPLE	SOLUTION
"You just said what? Did what?"	"You've got to be kidding me!"	Either . . . Push back and escalate or take a break and CALM down

HOW TO BREAK THE CYCLE OF FAMILY DYSFUNCTION

Dysfunctional anger can be passed down from generation to generation. Paulo shares:

My dad told us horrific stories of physical abuse when he was growing up. His father would beat him with sticks or anything else he could get his hands on. It seems he took all his anger out on him with an unleashed rage. No wonder he was so mean to me. It was learned.

Here are some steps to break the anger cycle in your life.

☐ **Become aware** of any past family destructive relationship patterns that have developed into habits and patterns for you in the present.

You have probably seen some areas where your upbringing is lacking. Notice them, take stock of how they have influenced you until the present. Ask yourself why certain members of your family may have been angry, harsh, cruel, or abusive.

☐ **Take ownership of your own actions,** attitudes, beliefs, and emotions in the here and now.

Yet, any deficiencies in our history are no excuse for us not to grow and move forward. This calls us to take control of our responses to our family dysfunctions. It is a conscious choice to say we will stop the cycle in this generation. That does not mean we compensate and provide no direction or discipline, but certainly not the abuses we may have observed.

☐ **Purposely observe,** compare, and contrast other families' interactions with how your family handles similar situations. Find a "hero" family.

☐ **Find someone around you** who is a good representation of the kind of family you'd like to have. Look for good role models of family leadership. Obviously, don't expect anyone to be perfect, just find a family that seems to function.

☐ **You can do internet searches on:**
- What makes up a functional family.
- Family roles or scripts.
- Adult attachment pain.
- Boundaries in relationships.
- Signs somebody may be manipulating in a relationship.
- Healthy Family Concepts. **(www.boundless.org)**

Share any family stories that have been shared about anger issues.

_____
_____
_____

Describe any destructive or toxic family relationships you might have.

_____
_____
_____

If you take ownership of your own emotions and reactions, how will that help you with your current anger?

_____
_____
_____

How did your family compare to any healthy families, or healthy principles you've observed?

_____
_____
_____
_____
_____
_____

WHAT REALLY ANGERS PEOPLE?

Check any boxes that are familiar to you.

☐ **Someone Stronger** takes over, takes control, overpowers them. This may create an overarching sense of or need to control others.

☐ **Suffering Losses** – someone takes something from them.

- Betrayal of trust.
- Loss of Innocence.
- Loss of Dignity.
- Possessions being stolen or taken.

☐ **Failed Expectations** – the current realities of life may not meet aspirations.

☐ **Feeling threatened, without options** – You feel your alternatives and choices are limited to what's being forced. Threats produce fear which produces a fight, flight, or freeze reaction.

- **Fight, to fight back** at someone who may be bigger and stronger. People do not usually fight back if they are convinced, they cannot win. Unless they plan ahead and prepare to fight, they will probably go to the next option.

- **Flight, to try and run from,** or avoid the person or situation. People can run all their lives because they were overpowered at an earlier time in their lives.

- **Freeze, to shut down** and be paralyzed to no action at all. When someone feels there are no options physically or emotionally, they may freeze up and not be able to leave the scene. Then, the abuse happens with no push back.

☐ **Other** _____.

Getting to the root of anger is important. Which of the anger drives can you relate to most? Why?

_____
_____
_____

When threatened, which of the fight, flight, or freeze is your typical reaction?

_____
_____
_____

For the anger of man does not produce the righteousness of God. James 1:20

If our anger does not work out God's righteousness, what should we do about it?

_____
_____
_____

THE HEART OF THE MATTER

The combination of one's **personality** (wiring or bent) mixed with observed and **learned behavior** (family systems) and **personal wounds** (past trauma or hurt) create an atmosphere where anger flourishes.

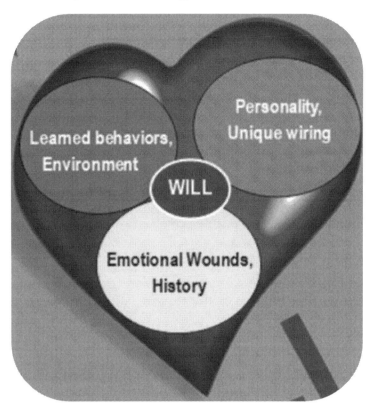

THE "HEART" COMBINATION

Personality. People tend to be either more task-oriented (actions and activities) or more people-oriented (relationships).

- **Lions/lionesses** naturally tend to control and react quickly.
- **Retrievers** tend to exaggerate and express their emotions openly.
- **Owls** tend to hold their feelings in until they can't take it any longer and implode.
- **Turtles** tend to hide and avoid confrontation until they can't take it any longer.

Personality refers to the unique patterns of thoughts, feelings, and behaviors that distinguish an individual from others. It is a product of both biology and environment, remaining fairly consistent throughout life.

Describe your personality:

_____
_____
_____

Share some of your learned behaviors concerning anger:

_____
_____
_____

List any personal wounds that have attributed to your anger:

_____
_____
_____

Think of some other ways you've seen that describe personality.

_____
_____
_____

What consistent characteristics make up your "uniqueness?"

_____
_____
_____

For instance, we might say, "She is generous, caring, and a bit of a perfectionist," or "They are loyal and protective of their friends."

The word "personality" originates from the Latin word persona, which referred to the theatrical masks worn by performers to play roles or disguise their identities. Most definitions of personality focus on the pattern of behaviors and characteristics that help predict and explain a person's actions. These characteristics include:

☐ **Consistency:** There is a recognizable order and regularity to behaviors. People tend to act in similar ways across various situations.

☐ **Psychological and Physiological:** Personality is a psychological construct, but it is also influenced by biological processes and needs.

☐ **Impact on Behaviors and Actions:** Personality influences how we move, respond, and act in our environment.

☐ **Multiple Expressions:** Personality is not only displayed in behavior but also in thoughts, feelings, close relationships, and other social interactions.

Ultimately, personality encompasses moods, attitudes, opinions, and is most clearly expressed in interactions with others.

(verywellmind.com, britannica.com, merriam-webster.com, apa.org, psychcentral.com)

Describe some of the "persona masks" you put on and wear out in public.

1. _____
   _____
   _____

2. _____
   _____
   _____

3. _____
   _____
   _____

What purposes does each one serve?

_____
_____
_____

What external factors have helped shape your personality?

_____
_____
_____

☐ **Learned Behaviors.**

We live what we learn. If growing up your family was chaotic, argumentative, and non-communicating, it is likely we will react the same way in a confrontation. If there was a belief system like one of the following, these can show up in our present lifestyle.

- "You are never allowed to express your anger."
- "I can get angry and yell, etc. but you cannot."
- "Children are to be seen and never heard."
- "Don't you ever dare question or ask why."

☐ **Personal Wounds**

Past trauma or hurt can create an atmosphere where anger flourishes. Emotional and/or physical trauma can greatly influence the expression of one's personality and approach to learned behaviors. When a person has been hurt over and again, they may develop a victim mentality.

Master these concepts to move forward.

- **EMOTIONAL TANK:** The importance of seeing yourself and others around you as emotional tanks that receive deposits or withdrawals.
- **PROBLEM SOLVING:** Learn to work with people to solve problems.
- **TRIGGER SHEETS:** Write out your experiences on the "Trigger Sheet."
- **FAMILY CYCLE:** Break the family cycle of dysfunction.

 Since we can now look at people as emotional tanks, we constantly get to help fill them up, or we may mistakenly make withdrawals. Now, we will look at the **CALM** method of anger management and begin with the letter C, CONNECT the dots.

How were anger, arguments, and fights handled in your family when you were growing up?

_____

_____

_____

_____

Describe any emotional or physical wounds you still carry from abuse or dysfunction in your home:

_____

_____

_____

_____

Which concept (s) do you believe you have now mastered from this chapter?

_____

_____

_____

_____

MYSELF IN PARTS

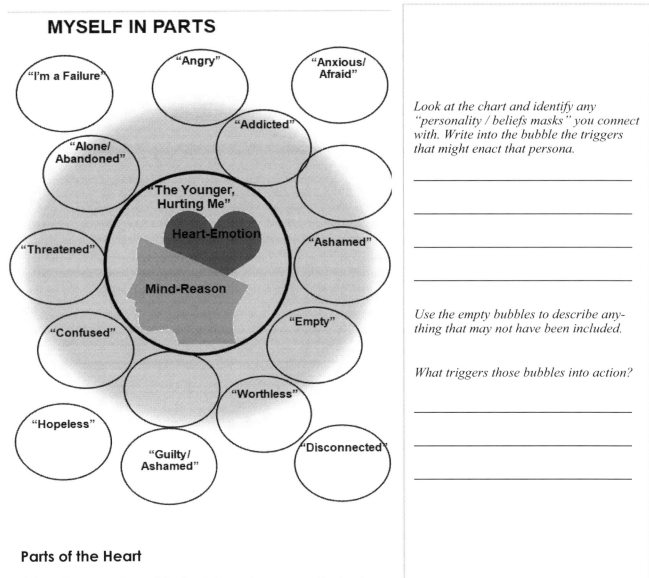

Look at the chart and identify any "personality / beliefs masks" you connect with. Write into the bubble the triggers that might enact that persona.

_____

_____

_____

_____

Use the empty bubbles to describe anything that may not have been included.

What triggers those bubbles into action?

_____

_____

_____

Parts of the Heart

It is not unusual, and in fact, it makes sense that when we are dealing with overwhelming issues, our brain may seek to deal with it in parts rather than the whole.

These "parts of the heart" may serve different functions like protecting and deflecting. It can be a way to avoid painful memories and experiences. Unfortunately, this avoidance may create many other problems.

CONNECT THE DOTS

FIVE
CONNECT THE DOTS

OBJECTIVE

Establish the concept of boundaries with anger management.

What you will learn in this chapter:

- Connect the dots of past and present anger triggers.
- Several myths and facts about anger.
- Ways to provide safety in relationships.
- The use of code words with the cliff metaphor.

Devonte and Shanna's Story

Devonte and Shanna have been together for over a year. They feel they are a great couple. Shanna shares, "But now some time has passed, and we have become comfortable in the relationship. Someone might say 'the honeymoon is over.' Devonte keeps making these cruel jabs at me, and it really hurts. I do not feel 'safe' with him anymore."

Shanna had been in an abusive relationship before and promised herself that she would never be hurt like that again. So, she has shut down and emotionally and physically locked Devonte out, distancing herself inside the home. This causes Devonte to become more angry and even vindictive.

After months of counseling, "D." has learned to:

- Recognize his vengeful actions.
- Accept just how hurtful his words have been towards Shanna.
- See that lashing out on her was not working or causing Shanna to want to get closer to him.
- He must apologize for his "locker room" behaviors.
- He needs to make a serious commitment never to be abusive toward her again.
- He signed the behavioral contract which helped rebuild trust in the relationship.

Remember, we are never trying to excuse behaviors, we are seeking to understand the "whys" of where they have come from. Dr. Paul

When you let anger get the best of you, it brings out the worst in you.

Do Shanna's reactions seem justified in your opinion?

_____
_____
_____

What concerns would you have for Devonte?

_____
_____
_____
_____
_____
_____

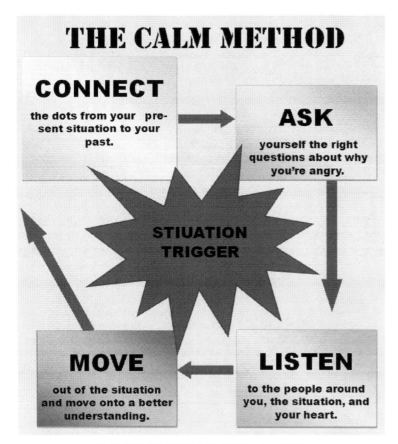

CONNECTING THE DOTS

Triggered and Fired Up!

When the human body is in an angered state, the sympathetic nervous system and the muscular system prepare for a physical attack. Muscles tense, blood pressure, and heart rate raise.

These changes may have once been a great advantage for someone in a hunter / gathering society. However, in this day and age they can be harmful to one's health. In addition to an increase in heart rate and blood pressure the levels of hormones, adrenaline, and noradrenalin all increase as well.

Serotonin levels of the brain can affect anger in a negative way. Hypothalamic nerve cells send messages deep into the brain causing the kidneys to pump large doses of adrenaline and cortisol into the bloodstream. Cortisol helps the body maintain its blood pressure. Having excess amounts of it pumped into the body causes the fluctuation of blood pressure while someone is angry. (Woodruff, 2018)

In our graphic, we see 4 boxes. In the center is the triggering situation:

- *person,*
- *problem,*
- *pain, or*
- *pressure.*

When a triggering situation happens, we need to CALM down.

Why is "Connecting the Dots" from our present triggering situation to any similar past events important?

_____
_____
_____
_____
_____

What could "Connecting the Dots" possibly do for us?

_____
_____
_____
_____
_____

SNAKE OR STICK?

It would be like walking out of your front door and seeing something that appeared to be a very large black snake under your vehicle. Your entire nervous system would go into either run or attack mode. (fight, flight, or freeze) Then, as you get closer to the car you see that it is a stick with a shadow that appears to be a snake. Yet, your system is still in a hyperactive, or hyper-alert mode. If you were to continue to be in that mode for a long time it would become a **chronic problem**.

What follows are some of the Myths and Facts about how we handle this sense of alertness and anger. Check and see which applies to you.

MYTHS AND FACTS ABOUT ANGER

☐ **Myth One:** "I shouldn't 'hold in' my anger. It's healthy to vent and let it out any way I want."

Fact: Outbursts and tirades only fuel the fire and reinforce your anger. If anger is released without boundaries, serious consequences may ensue. Anger tends to grow if left to itself without any form of restraint.

☐ **Myth Two:** "Anger, aggression, and intimidation will help me earn respect and get what I want."

Fact: True power doesn't come from bullying others; it comes from earning respect through positive actions and being a good example. People may obey rules through intimidation, but they will have no motivation in themselves to continue once the pressure is gone.

☐ **Myth Three:** "I can't help myself. Anger isn't something I could ever control."

Fact: You _can_ control how you express your anger because you can control yourself. Once you begin taking charge of your angry responses in small ways you will graduate to be able to control it in larger situations and circumstances.

☐ **Myth Four:** "Anger management is about forcing yourself to suppress your anger."

Fact: Never getting angry is not a good goal either. It is **how you direct your anger** that matters. (adapted from helpguide.org)

Describe a time you misread a situation that could have produced a great amount of stress, (snake that wasn't a snake) later to find it wasn't what you thought (a shadow).

_____

_____

_____

_____

_____

_____

Which of the myths do you relate to most and why?

_____

_____

_____

Who have you known who tried to earn respect by intimidation? Did it work for that person?

_____

_____

_____

What eventually happens when a person suppresses their anger, pretending it doesn't exist?

_____

_____

_____

_____

IT MAKES MY BLOOD BOIL!

When a cartoon character gets angry, steam comes out the ears, red creeps over the body from head to toe and there may even be an explosion or two. It's not as entertaining to watch in real life. The state of anger causes physical reactions. The response varies from person to person, but some symptoms include teeth grinding, fist clenching, flushing, prickly sensations, numbness, sweating, muscle tensions and temperature changes (Tavris).

ANGER TRIGGERS

What Pushes Your Buttons?
(Check any boxes that apply)

☐ **Correcting a wrong.** "It frustrates me when I see a problem and try to correct the person, - especially if they are not willing to listen or change."

☐ **Maintaining a relationship.** "I get angry when I'm trying to keep the relationship together, but the other party isn't really trying."

☐ **Demonstrating power**. "When people disrespect me, or don't listen, I take it as a personal affront that has to be corrected at any cost." Included in the power issue can be the struggle to gain and/or maintain control.

☐ **Social injustice.** "It's frustrating to see injustice in the world and not see people fixing it, or not be a part of fixing it."

☐ **Violated rights.** "It makes me very angry if someone tries to take away any of my personal rights or something I believe I have a right to."

☐ Other _____

Which of the above (if any) drives you to become angry most often?

➡ We have seen our strategic goal of becoming assertive and finding a place of calm. We looked at more possible triggers. Now, let's move into what it means to provide safety in our relationships.

---

*Describe your favorite **"angry cartoon character"** growing up. Why was he or she so angry?*

_____

_____

_____

_____

Which of the anger triggers troubles you the most?

_____

_____

_____

Why?

_____

_____

_____

_____

HOW TO PROVIDE SAFETY IN A RELATIONSHIP

Gerald and Lisa sit in front of the counselor. Gerald says, "Okay, what is it you wanted to tell me that had to wait until we got to the counselor's office?" Lisa shares, "Well, I wanted to tell you this while we were in an environment I could trust . . . I just don't feel **safe** with you any more."

"Safe?" Gerald yells. "What the hell are you talking about. I've never hit you or hurt you. How could you ever feel 'unsafe' around me?"

The One of the first and most important steps in dealing with anger and relationships is to let go of any sense of revenge or punishment of people in your life. It may be that in the past you have made it a habit to do your best to get even with people for disagreements or push back

"When I did _____ it was because I was angry because I felt _____."

What I will do differently next time is

_____

THE POWER OF CODE WORDS

In the middle of a tense, serious, and complicated situation the right code word can bring a moment of levity. The funnier the word is, the better. **Code words:**

CODE WORDS SHOULD BE:

- **Simple:** If the code word is simple and light-hearted it will be memorable.
- **Concise:** It can reduce an entire discussion and explanation into a word or two.
- **Agreed:** All parties must agree on the word, and the right use of it.
- **Consistent:** It must be used every time they are needed to provide a safe environment.
- **Safe:** It must produce the desired safety result.

What is Lisa trying to get across to Gerald?

_____

_____

Do you think it worked?

_____

Understanding the importance of "safety" in a relationship, list anything about your attitudes and/or behaviors that may have made people feel:

- *condescending*
- *criticized,*
- *fearful,*
- *threatened,*
- *endangered.*

Please explain:

_____

_____

_____

Given your situation, think of several possible "code words" that would change your state of mind if the person closest to you were to use them.

_____

_____

What will be your greatest challenge is using a "code word?"

_____

_____

It's important to remember that you can have code words and all the tools necessary to build a good relationship, but the do no good unless you practice and use them.

THE CLIFF METAPHOR

Along with code words, to develop safety and trust in a relationship, we use the "Wall and the Cliff" illustration. If the wall of a mountain is the safest place to be, then the goal is to keep close to it. The wall is a 0, no stress-no danger zone.

The Wall: This represents total safety, measuring 0 anger and stress zone. The main goal is to stay as close as possible to the wall (safety zone) as possible.

The Road: This is your relationship pathway. It is filles with twists and turns.

The Cliff: This is the most extreme consequence, measuring 10.

Bill and Linda's Story

Bill had a terrible outburst with his wife, Linda. He has done this more than once. He was yelling, threatening her, and put his fist through the wall. Their neighbors called the police, and Bill was arrested. The next week, in counseling, they begin to rebuild trust in the relationship. The Counselor taught them the **"Cliff Metaphor"** with **"Code Words."**

☐ **THE SAFETY ZONE.**

Bill and Linda decide what each zone should be and what a desired consequence would be should things get out of hand. One of the goals is to help Bill become aware of his aggressive behaviors and have an alternative should he begin to feel out of control.

Bill and Linda describe their "safety zone" as "couch time" together after the children are in bed. They get to debrief and talk about things that matter.

What does your wall of safety look like? Is it a state of mind? Is it a physical place?

_____
_____
_____

The road is the path you're on. Describe your "relationship path" in a few words:

_____
_____
_____
_____

What is your cliff, or "worst case consequence" scenario?

_____
_____
_____
_____

Share some of the ways you will avoid falling off the cliff:

_____
_____
_____
_____
_____
_____

CODE WORDS.

They decided to use the code word **"popcorn"** to get Bill's attention anytime he might start drifting away from the "wall of safety." They arrive home, and the next day, Bill reverts to some of his old behaviors.

0 = safety zone, calm, no stress. The goal is to stay as close to the safety zone as possible.

TRIGGER: Bill and Linda have a disagreement over what time their daughter should come home from a date with her friends.

3 = Bill gets agitated and raises his voice. Linda says, "popcorn."

Consequence Response. Bill is supposed to leave the room for 15 minutes to cool down. He leaves, and realizes the situation isn't worth getting this angry. He works through the **CALM** method, (you will see this later). Then he comes back calmed down. Situation resolved. **Or...**

5 = Bill starts trying to guilt and manipulate Linda and gets louder because Linda has asked him to take a hike. She calmly says "Popcorn." He is angry.

Consequence Response. Bill leaves the house for a few hours and comes back. He realizes he is in real emotional trouble. He calls a friend and then works through the **CALM** method. He comes back home calmed down. Situation resolved. **Or . . .**

7 = Bill begins threatening Linda and throws a coffee mug at the wall. He starts pacing the floor and calling Linda offensive names. Linda says, "Popcorn Bill," several times.

Consequence Response. Bill hesitantly leaves and goes to his parent's home one hour away to stay until their next counseling appointment. They talk about his situation, and he calls his friend to talk. He works through the **CALM** method. He and Linda meet at the Counselor's office the next week to review each part of the situation together calmly. Bill again, makes a commitment to the plan. Situation resolved. **Or . . .**

10 = They are at the edge of the cliff. The worst possible case scenario. This ends up in a long-term separation, divorce, etc.

If you make it your goal to keep to the "0" (safety zone wall) as much as possible, everything should be fine. What should you do if you stray from it?

_____
_____
_____

What is Bill's biggest mistake?

_____
_____
_____

List the poor decisions Bill makes as he slips away from the "wall of safety."

_____
_____
_____
_____

Does getting to a 9 or v10 scenario have to be the end of the road for a relationship?

_____
_____
_____

YOUR TURN – CLIFFS AND CODES

What is your "Code Word?"

_____

☐ **0 -2 =** Describe your calm, no-stress, safety zone.

_____

☐ Describe a posible TRIGGER that could posible disrupt your safe, peaceful zone.

_____

☐ **Describe a 3 – 4 zone =** What negative actions might you take that would move you closer to the danger cliff, and away from the peaceful, safety zone (wall).

_____

Consequence Response. What consequences to moving away from the wall of safety might cause you to return back to the safety zone (wall)?

_____

☐ **Describe a 5 -7 =** What negative actions might you take that would move you closer to the danger cliff, and even further away from the peaceful, safety zone (wall).

_____

Consequence Response. What consequences to moving away from the wall of safety might cause you to return back to the safety zone (wall)?

_____

☐ **Describe a 7 -9 =** What negative actions might you take that would move you closer to the danger cliff, and away from the peaceful, safety zone (wall).

_____

Consequence Response. What consequences to moving even further away from the wall of safety mifght cause you to return basck to the safety zone back at the wall?

_____

☐ **Describe a 10 =** What does the very worst, "falling of the cliff," consequence look like.

DOMESTIC VIOLENCE
PERSONAL SAFETY CONTRACT

Everyone has the right to be safe!

Date: _____

This agreement is made between _____ and _____. The purpose of this contract is to provide safety for everyone involved. By signing this agreement, we are both making a commitment toward providing a safe environment for all parties involved.

The incident that created the need for this contract was:

_____

_____

Check any boxes that apply.

- ☐ Emotional abuse, belittling, name calling, shamed.
- ☐ Physical Violence. (hit, slap, punch, etc.)
- ☐ Destruction of personal property.
- ☐ Verbal threats.
- ☐ Making people feel afraid.
- ☐ Throwing things.
- ☐ Threatening self-harm.
- ☐ Abusive words/name-calling.
- ☐ Forced sex. (sexual advances)
- ☐ Other _____.
- ☐ Other _____.

➡ "The following steps represent my plan for increasing safety and preparing in advance for the possibility of further issues or violence. Although I do not have control over my partner's violence or reactions, I do have a choice about how to respond to him/her and how to best get myself and/or my children to safety."

STRATEGIC AGREEMENTS

1. If you _____ become angry, escalate with anger, or become frustrated, I will use the code word _____ which should cause you to step away from the situation. If you follow the plan, the problem is currently resolved.

2. If we have an argument, we will move to an open area or room with an exit away from any type of weapons, or danger where I can easily leave if I choose to.

3. I have a well-planned exit. If I decide to leave, I will go to a safe place.

4. I will keep my car keys close by and ready in order to leave quickly if necessary.

5. I will tell _____ about the abuse/situation and request that he/she call the police if he/she hears suspicious noises coming from my home, or if I ask them to do so.

6. I will teach the children how to use the phone to contact the police, fire department, 911, etc.

7. I will use _____ as my code word with my children and friends so they can call for help.

8. I will use my judgment and intuition. If the situation gets very serious, I will do whatever it takes to be safe and get out of harm's way.

Signed _____   Date _____

Signed _____   Date _____

Witness _____   Date _____

Master these concepts to move forward.

- **CONNECTION:** Connect the dots between your current issues and anything linked to your past.
- **AWARENESS:** Become aware of and sensitive to your personal triggers.
- **SAFETY:** Provide safety in your relationships with code words and boundaries.

Which concept (s) do you believe you have now mastered from this chapter?

6
ASK THE RIGHT QUESTIONS

SIX
ASK THE RIGHT QUESTIONS

OBJECTIVE

Practice filtering thoughts, feelings, and actions by asking the right questions.

What you will learn in this chapter:

- The importance of asking calming questions during an angry event.
- Whether your natural bent is toward fight, flight, or freeze.
- Problem-solving with the 5 why questions.

Jamal and Mikala's Story

Jamal spend 10 years serving in the military. He went through some rough times, but believes he is a "true survivor." After returning from several high-risk deployments, he got a job as a police officer. He loves his job and is really dedicated to serving the community. Unfortunately, there is one big problem. He tends to bring his work home with him.

"He lines our three children up for inspection and treats them like they're criminals sometimes," Mikala complains. "He seems to be taking his work frustrations out on me and the kids, especially our oldest 13-yrear-old son."

Jamal feels he is making his family become "responsible citizens" and does these things for their own good. Mikala feels he takes things to far and their son is becoming very rebellious.

Jamal would do well to learn:

- Once he arrives home, he is no longer on duty. He needs to change his mindset when his hand touches the door knob.
- His wife and children do not deserve to be treated like criminals.
- If he does not find positive ways to bond with his son, he is going to lose him.
- He and Mikala should get help.

Just because I don't fight back, doesn't mean I'm weak. It means I'm mature enough to know that anger won't solve anything.

How difficult is it for you to not push back, or fight back with people or struggle to have the last word?

_____
_____
_____
_____

What questions would you like to ask Jamal about his situation?

_____
_____
_____
_____

What could Mikala do to help the situation?

_____
_____
_____
_____

What might you add to the concepts Jamal would do well to learn?

_____
_____
_____
_____

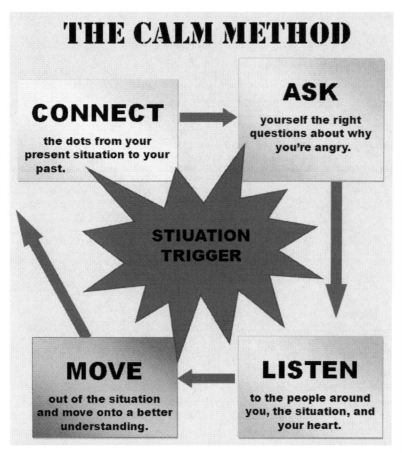

> "Most misunderstandings in the world could be avoided if people would simply take the time to ask, 'What else could this mean?'" Shannon Alder

How could seeking the "deeper meaning" behind anger make things different?

_____
_____
_____

We have gone from "Connecting the Dots," to "Asking the Right Questions."

Think of three questions you should ask yourself before responding during a triggering situation.

_____
_____
_____
_____
_____
_____

➤ Remember, one of the keys to calming down a hyper-alert brain is to take a minute before reacting. A good way to do this is to ask ourselves some thought-provoking questions.

Have you every tried to "take a minute" before reacting? If so, how did that work out?

_____
_____
_____

CALMING QUESTIONS

There are numerous questions you can ask yourself to help you handle a potentially anger-causing situation. For example:

- How **important** is it to me to win this argument, etc.? (Learn to choose your battles well. If most every day is a major battle, then something is probably wrong).

- Is what I am thinking or feeling **appropriate**? Does my reaction match the situation?

- Is it really about this situation or something else? (Does your anger go deeper towards a previous **similar** situation?)

- What can I do to create an outcome that I desire without getting upset? (If you know what you would like to see happen, maybe you can get there without rage).

- Is it better to allow an **outcome** that I do not particularly desire for the sake of peaceful resolution? Comedian Jeff Allen once said something I will never forget.

"Do you want to be happy, or do you want to be right?"

If we are constantly competing and fighting for our "**perfectly right opinion**," chances are we will end up alone at the end of the day. Even if we are right, is it worth alienating ourselves from others and creating enemies all around us? So, it would be best to learn to listen to people and ask ourselves some tough questions before reacting to a triggered situation!

Improving your anger control skills is a process of listening and asking the right questions.

This is not something that you will be good at overnight. There are several things that you must work on in order to be skilled in the art of anger management. Learn to identify your feelings and thoughts, including your physiological feelings that indicate anger. (remember the TFA chart)

Learn to evaluate any negative thought patterns that may be contributing. Analyze your feelings and options that have not worked well in the past to determine better ways of handling potentially anger-inducing situations. Learn to empathize with others and understand how things must feel from their perspective. Especially, work on your problem-solving skills to allow yourself a greater number of options other than anger and frustration. (Woodruff, 2018)

Develop your own questions that fit the following key words:

IMPORTANT

_____

APPROPRIATE

_____

SIMILAR

_____

OUTCOME

_____

Which of the questions do you think you could most easily remember in a crisis moment?

_____

How do you respond to the idea that you can either be happy or be right?

_____

_____

_____

Do you tend to be a "fighter" or a "flighter"?

"Fiighters" (or runners) tend to run from conflicts. They may avoid conflict at any cost. The concept of "ghosting" is the social media way of avoiding issues. You simply ignore the other person's existence, unfriend them, block them, and cancel their existence. The unfortunate problem with this is that relationships are often forged and bonded through conflict. The "flight type of person" may miss many opportunities for growth, compromise, and benefits of working through differences.

"Fighters" can be complicated as well. Once they dig their heels into an argument or skirmish, it can be very difficult to get them to shift gears. They may take their position personally as an afront to their existence when questioned or when someone disagrees. This can take place over days, hours, minutes, or even seconds!

I once had a good friend who could go from zero to 200 miles an hour with his anger in seconds. When he got to that point, with that type of anger, it was almost impossible to get him to slow down or stop and think about the situation. When his primal, what we called his "monster brain" would kick in, he would refuse to back down. He goes into a blind rage and can't even remember what he's done some times.

Because of it, he has left a long list of people with whom he has burned bridges. Unfortunately, he doesn't recognize it as the problem it really is.

Let's slow the whole thing down and learn to ask ourselves questions about our situation.

THE 5 WHY QUESTIONS

This is a question-asking technique used to explore the cause-and-effect relationships underlying a particular problem.

It's just as it sounds: A discussion of the unexpected event or challenge that follows one train of thought to its logical conclusion by asking "Why?" five times to get to the root of what happened.

It's important to note that the purpose of the 5 whys isn't to place blame, but rather to uncover the root cause of why something unexpected occurred. Additionally, it helps a team create small, incremental steps so that the same issue doesn't happen again (to anyone).

Do you tend to be a "fighter" or a "flighter"? Please explain...

_____

_____

_____

Fighting can come in many ways.
- *push back*
- *aggression*
- *yelling*
- *Other*

_____

_____

_____

Answering your "WHY" as to the reasoning behind your stress and anger is key. So far, what have you discovered about yourself and your personal journey?

_____

_____

_____

5-WHY FLOWCHART

First. A trigger happens. It may come from a question from someone, an issue, a problem arises.

Second. Identify the problem, give it a name.

Third. Identify the causes. Ask, "WHY did this happen?" WHAT is the logical root problem?"

Fourth. WHAT are some possible solutions for each cause? Make a list of all possibilities.

https://buffer.com/resources/5-whys-process/

LET'S MAKE IT REAL

An example: "My wife and I are angry with each other!"
Why?

- ☐ **Why?** Because she asked me where I had been. **Why?**
- ☐ **Why?** Because I was late again. **Why?**
- ☐ **Why?** Because I stopped at the bar. **Why?**
- ☐ **Why?** Because I drank a lot of beer to escape. **Why?**
- ☐ **Why?** Because she's afraid of what might happen next.

The following are some questions that can lead to solutions.

"**Why** have I shown anger in such a way that others have become afraid of me, or feel "unsafe" around me?

"**How** can I learn to express my anger in a way that will not leave me feeling helpless and powerless?"

"**When** I'm angry, why haven't I clearly communicated my position without becoming defensive or attacking?"

"**What** risks and losses might I face if I become clearer and more <u>assertive</u>?"

"**If getting angry is not working, WHAT can I do differently?"**

This is a review of the typical angry episode and its core components when a person objectively works through it.

Triggers come from many sources and are most often unexpected and often unwelcomed.

Giving our triggers a name can help in the process.

Examples:

"I'm having a ____."

"It's the monster mash."

"The Hulk is about to show up."

Others:

_____

_____

Then, we begin asking questions. Who, what, when, where, and WHY?

Which of the "why" questions do you relate to the most? Why?

_____

_____

It is most important to ask the following question to discover the "why" the problem exists:

"WHAT is the problem?

_____

_____

Whose problem is it, who should it belong to?"

_____

_____

Master these concepts to move forward.

- **ASK:** Ask yourself calming questions when you separate from an angry episode.
- **CHOOSE:** Learn to choose your battles well so you don't fight to always be right.
- **ATTACK THE PROBLEM:** Define and attack the problem, not people.

➡ We have **Connected the Dots**, and learned to **Ask** the right questions, now we can Listen to the people around us and listen to our own selves about our situation.

Which concept (s) do you believe you have now mastered from this chapter?

_____
_____
_____
_____

7 LISTEN TO PEOPLE

SEVEN
LISTEN TO PEOPLE

OBJECTIVE
Practice the power of active listening.

What you will learn in this chapter:

- To listen before reacting during an anger event.
- To follow the rules of "fighting fair" during an argument.
- Cooling down techniques for listening.
- Avoid escalating toward possible violence.

Jake's Story

Jake had a bad habit. He would often cut people off when they were talking so he could get his opinion into the conversation. He was unaware of just how off-putting this was, and that people were avoiding him. He notv only cut people off, then he would have to have the last word in the conversation to prove he was right.

This all came to a head when someone at work told him he was a "smartass" and needed to stop disrespecting him by cutting him off. Jake went off on the co-worker and was written up for it. He was so compulsive, he wouldn't listen to the criticisms of people around him.

Jake needed to come to several understandings:

- He was showing signs of adult ADHD; this needed to be dealt with.
- He was not allowed to share his opinions as a child and was overly anxious about it now as an adult.
- This happened in several scenarios of his life, at home, family events, and now at work.
- He needed to learn to "wait his turn" to share his opinions when appropriate.
- It is important to "mind your own business" at times.
- This behavior could get him into serious trouble with certain people.

"There is nothing that can be done with anger that cannot be done better without it." Dallas Willard

Describe someone you know who is somewhat like Jake.

_____

_____

_____

What kinds of things might make someone like Jake as this way?

_____

_____

_____

What other advice might you give Jake?

_____

_____

_____

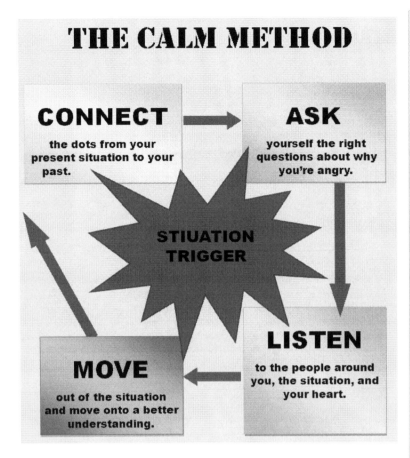

WAIT A MINUTE

Have you ever hit the send button on an email or text and instantly regretted it? Never to return, no do over, no opportunity to take back what you said. Someone sent me a scathing text once. When I called to find out what was going on, their response was, "Oh, I sent that to you by accident." Sure, but the information they sent must have been what they were really thinking!

 Listening and speaking is like that. It's wise to monitor our words and reactions. They say that's why we have two ears and one mouth, right?

CONNECT

We learned to "Connect the Dots" when we're angry.

ASK

Then we were careful to "Ask the Right Questions" about why we are angry and how to deal with it.

LISTEN

Now we will "Listen to the people around us." As we listen to our own hearts and those around us, we begin to get a clearer picture of our current situation.

Describe a moment you hastily did something only to instantly regret it.

_____
_____
_____

What was the outcome?

_____
_____
_____

LISTEN AND THINK BEFORE YOU ACT OR SPEAK!

Common Communications Mistakes.
(Check any boxes that apply to you)

☐ **"We think we are the center of the universe, It's all about me."** This is when the conversation revolves around one person's feelings and perspectives. It's only fair for both parties to have a voice and share in a discussion.

☐ **"We forget to breathe."** When under duress, most often people's breathing is altered. Deep breathing can calm down an intense situation, and lower stress.

☐ **"We escalate the situation."** An argument can quickly go up higher and higher with varying degrees of tension. It is better to interrupt the pattern before it escalates.

☐ **"We have unclear needs or expectations."** If one of the two parties does not, or cannot describe what they desire, or need in the situation, it becomes hard to come to a healthy solution. Expectations are often a secret, hidden language ofv thev heart that need to revealed.

☐ **"Being judgmental."** Once one of the two people involved pronounces judgement (you always say that, or you never do this) it tends to shut the communication down.

☐ **"Acting passive or aggressive rather than assertive."** A passive reaction is when one of or both people stop responding and start planning any form of revenge. This can be a silent treatment or ignoring the other person's existence.

☐ **"It's all or nothing attitude."** This is when one of the parties shuts the conversation down with a statement that their way is the only way, and their conclusion is the only one that can be acceptable. In their opinion, this makes them always right and everyone else wrong.

These should be avoided as much as possible.
Here are some ground rules for any discussion or argument. They will he4lp keep the situation safe and should be agreed on before anything comes up.

---

*Which of the common communication mistakes are you sure you **do not** engage in?*

_____
_____
_____

Why do you do well with that one (s)?

_____
_____
_____
_____

Which of the common mistakes do you struggle with most?

_____
_____
_____

Why that one(s)?

_____
_____
_____
_____

LEARNING HOW TO FIGHT FAIR

We all get into arguments at one time or another. Having pre-determined rules for how to **"fight fair"** can provide an atmosphere of safety and help avoid situations getting out of hand.

☐ **Have pre-established boundaries to provide security.** People need to feel safe to share their feelings, thoughts, and responses without repercussion. The following are boundary commitments that provide safety in any relationship.

- "I will never hit you, throw things toward (at) you, or break things in anger."
- "I will not scream at you (especially not during a fight)."
- "I will not use malicious words that demean or insult you."
- "I will not fight to be right, trying to have the last word."
- "I will not link this argument with past skirmishes."
- "I will not use 'NEVER or ALWAYS.'"
- "I will not try to 'read your mind,' saying what I believe you're thinking."
- "I will let you finish your words before I take my turn."

☐ **Use the "DRIVE THROUGH" method.** To listen instead of just hearing; you can repeat back to the other person what you just heard them say to develop clarity. It's like going through the drive through at a fast-food restaurant. You tell the little microphone what you want and the person on the other end repeats back to you what you just ordered. If somehow, they got the order wrong, then you're able to clarify it.

☐ **Learn "what if's" compromising.** Good communications and fairness in arguments requires the development of options to resolve the situation. Having different alternatives to resolve a situation creates great security because when there is only one alternative and either party does not like it, then there is a problem. Seeking to meet somewhere in the middle with various options for success can be of great help.

☐ **Listen to the "HEART" of the person's frustrations.** If you slow things down in an argument and really look at the other person and ask them what's going on in their heart, you may get an opportunity to see what's really happening. If you can ask simple questions about their heart it can help you get to the root of the matter.

Why is it important to "fight fair" when in an argument.

_____
_____
_____

List any boundaries you would add to provide security.

_____
_____
_____

What's your favorite fast-food restaurant?

How well do they do with the "drive thru method?"

_____
_____

List any boundaries you would add to provide security.

_____
_____
_____

You can ask:
- *Are you afraid?*
- *Do you feel threatened?*
- *Are you offended?*

☐ **Reinterpret the situation.** One person said that every time they're cut off in traffic, they imagine that the individual who ran in front of them is in a hurry to get to the hospital because their wife is having a baby, or someone was just tragically hurt. For them, this instantly took away the sting of being cut off in traffic. Think of the situation differently, with compassion and concern.

☐ **You can devaluate** the stimuli by minimizing the trigger. Your initial response to any trigger can be explosive. If you make it a habit to shrink or minimize the trigger you may be able to better control your reactions to it. Pretend it's not nearly as big as it felt when it first hit you. Shrink it down to a smaller size.

☐ **Maximize possible harmful outcomes and consequences.** If you even exaggerate the possible negative results of releasing your anger and saying things that might be harmful, it may help you be able to take charge of the situation and your internal responses.

☐ **Come to a "logical conclusion."**

Most people want to come to a resolution in an argument. This should not mean that one or the other person wins, or guess the last word in. It means that there is a resolution to the problem that was presented in such a way that a positive outcome can be reached.

- "50/50. Sometimes we're both right, sometimes we're both wrong."
- "I can let this go even if I don't think I'm wrong."
- "I'd rather be happy than be right."
- "I'm choosing my battles well, and this is not a major one."
- "I only have one enemy, and you are not it."

*How could you **reinterpret** an angry situation that would provide compassion, patience, and clarity to it?*

_____
_____
_____

If you devalue the trigger and maximize the consequences, how might that help you come to a logical conclusion about your anger?

_____
_____
_____

Which of the "logical conclusions" can you see yourself using right away?

_____
_____
_____

COOLING DOWN

A "cool down" is when you simply leave the situation, get a handle on your feelings, and return to handle things more objectively. This may be what you need to do when you feel your physiological symptoms of anger. Get up and move out.

So, if the best thing to do when things heat up is to step away, what are you to do while you're away? Here are some good suggestions for cooling down from a heated situation.

☐ **Talk to yourself.** Talk yourself through it. Reason yourself into a calmer state. Reminding yourself not to take things personally. Talk yourself through the situation from the other person's perspective.

☐ **Meditate.** Meditation and relaxation exercises can help you relax and diffuse some of your anger. The physiological state you are in when you are relaxed is incompatible with the physiological state you are in when you are angry. Exercises can help the state of relaxation to be dominant, so you can handle the situation appropriately. Simply put, **breathe.**

☐ **Distract yourself.** Daydreaming and positive fantasizing are useful tools to distract you from anger when you are not actively listening to someone. For example, if you are asked to do a task that you find unfair and resent doing it and you feel yourself beginning to get angry as you do the work. Fantasizing and daydreaming may be a good tool while you complete the task to keep you in a positive state if there are no safety issues involved. (Woodruff, 2018)

➡ **Note:** Be aware that running from issues does not work in the long run. Neither do constant distractions. Moving out of an escalating scenario for a few moments to calm it down can be successful. Just remember, you will still have the problem to solve from which you took a break.

There are options for "cool down" activities. Choose which one you like the most and explain how you will use it.

_____

_____

_____

How does running from your issues complicate your life?

_____

_____

Why don't distractions, or diverting your attention not work?

_____

_____

RECOGNIZING THE POTENTIAL FOR VIOLENCE

How to recognize if you're becoming aggressive.
(check any boxes that apply to you)

☐ **Threatening people.** You don't mind threatening people to get them to move into action and do what you want.

☐ **Harshness.** People tell you that you're mean and hurtful, but you don't see it.

☐ **Shifting Blame.** You find it easy to blame people for their mistakes to shame or embarrass them toward change. They may accuse you of "gaslighting," blaming them somehow for something you have done.

☐ **Holding a grudge.** It's hard to let go of an offense when you feel you've been wronged. (Tafrate and Kassinove, 2019)

Rate yourself on the following common mistakes people make in an argument. What can you do to better this mistake?

- "It's all about me."
- "I forget to breathe."
- "I escalate."
- "I don't have clear needs or expectations."
- "I can be judgmental."
- "I tend to be passive or aggressive rather than assertive."
- "With me it's all or nothing."

Which of the communications mistakes do you believe is the most dangerous to healthy relationships?

Let's practice the "drive through echo."

Master these concepts to move forward.

- **LISTEN:** Listen carefully to the people around you.
- **AVOID:** Avoid the common communication mistakes.
- **FIGHT FAIR:** Follow the rules of "Fighting Fair."
- **COOL DOWN:** Cool down in any stressful or angering situation.

 We have just discussed active listening to learn empathy for others. If a situation becomes heated, our best option may be to leave the scene for numerous reasons.

Describe 3 healthy boundaries you would be willing to begin to develop in your communications relating to anger.

"I will never _____ "

"I will not _____ "

"I will seek to _____ "

What is your takeaway from the information on active listening?

_____
_____
_____

Which concept (s) do you believe you have now mastered from this chapter?

_____
_____
_____

8
MOVE ON OR MOVE OUT

EIGHT
MOVE ON OR MOVE OUT

OBJECTIVE

Practice the power of moving out of an escalating situation.

What you will learn in this chapter:

- You have the personal power of choice no matter what your history or circumstance is.
- The strategic goals of anger management.
- When to move out of an angry situation.
- To evaluate your relationships to make further decisions.

Jay and Deb's Story

Jay and Deb were arguing a lot. Their fights would escalate to the point that Deb would try to leave, and Jay would keep her from getting out of the house. If somehow, she did, he would follow her and then stalk her wherever she went. He wouldn't even let her take her phone to call for help. (This can be considered kidnapping)

They sit before me and my office. We have been working together for months to build trust and repair some issues in their marriage. But last week they had an all-out war with each other over something that was very important to both of them. Now, they are at an impasse and have no idea what to do next.

He begins using phrases like, "this is indicative of how we're going." She begins using phrases like, "I don't feel like I can trust you anymore. I don't feel 'safe.'" These types of decorations are the death to any relationship.

They both need to understand:

- These skirmishes do not have to "define" the relationship.
- Kidnapping and stalking are serious behaviors.
- They have a long history together filled with many happy events and memories. '
- There will be more arguments in the future as there are in any relationship.
- One of the keys to a good relationship bis the ability to solve problems together.

Anger is the punishment we give ourselves for someone else's mistake.

Your anger is a reflection of you, not the person you are expressing it toward.

What were Jay's biggest mistakes?

_____

_____

_____

Describe any issues that have come up from the language they are both using.

_____

_____

_____

They feel like they've tried everything and now everything including counseling with me is a failure. I don't think so. So, I allowed them to fight and argue for a little while and then asked them abruptly to stop. Until then I tell them we're going to do something a little different today. I want you both to look at each other and repeat after me.

"I forgive you. Will you please forgive me?"

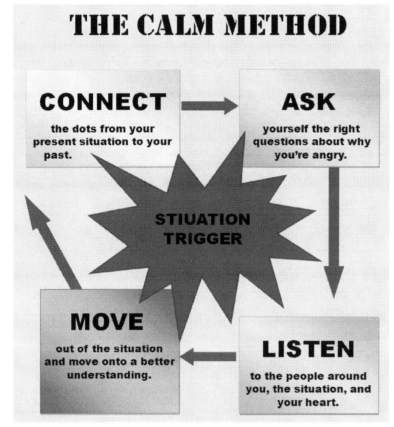

We get to the point that we realize that something has to move. Either a move, or shift in our hearts must take place or we must move away for a minute.

Forgiving a person who has offended, annoyed, broken, or hurt us is the best way to do that. Move our hearts toward them even though they do not deserve it.

What have you attempted before to help with your stress and/or anger?

_____
_____
_____
_____

Describe what forgiveness means to you.

_____
_____
_____
_____

Who might you need to forgive before you can move forward?

_____
_____
_____
_____

When and under what circumstances would you not forgive the people who have hurt you?

_____
_____
_____
_____

Forgiveness is a verb.

It means to stop feeling angry or resentful toward (someone) for an offense, flaw, or mistake. It means to cancel a debt.

So, forgiveness is the act of pardoning an offender; "to let the offense go." It is like a person who does not demand payment for a debt. Jesus used this comparison when he taught his followers to pray: "Forgive us our sins, as we forgive everyone who is in debt to us."

Forgiveness Facts

1. Everyone needs forgiveness.

No one is exempt. Everyone needs forgiveness at some time unless, of course you're perfect!

2. To find forgiveness, you must forgive others.

The truth is, you cannot give something you do not have. You cannot share forgiveness if you've never experienced forgiveness.

3. Bitterness (lack of forgiveness) is broken fellowship and requires repentance.

4. Forgive even if they don't ask or deserve it.

Forgiveness only requires one person while reconciliation requires two. You can forgive another person without any positive response from them. In that sense, forgiving may do more for you than it does the offender.

5. Forgiveness boundaries. There is no limit to forgiveness, it brings healing.

It is important to realize that forgiveness should be limitless, yet it still retains healthy boundaries. Forgiving someone does not mean you allow them right back in your life to re-offend. By their actions, they may have disqualified from the relationship.

What have you attempted before to help with your stress and/or anger?

_____

_____

_____

Describe what forgiveness means to you.

_____

_____

_____

_____

Who might you need to forgive before you can move forward?

_____

_____

_____

_____

Why is it so important to forgive other people's offenses first?

_____

_____

_____

When and under what circumstances would you not forgive the people who have hurt you?

_____

_____

_____

_____

Risks with the Lack of Forgiveness

Let's talk about this famous phrase: "Bitterness (unforgiveness) is like taking poison, hoping your offender will die from it."

Challenges and Hurdles to Forgiveness

- ☐ **Refusing** let go of the offense. There are people who enjoy living in their pain and may identify with it. The offense can take over their lives, making it feel impossible to let it go. Some people get to the point that they refuse to forgive.

- ☐ **Receiving** guilt and shame as your own. There are people who embrace the offense in the situation as if it were their fault. This false sense of guilt becomes a major hurdle because the focus is on the wrong person, the offended party rather than the offender.

- ☐ **Reliving** the offense over and over. A person \can replay the offense in their minds over and over again. They become so attached to it that it is overwhelming. Similar to PTSD, they relive the event or situations rather than deal with them properly.

- ☐ **Rejecting** the offender as a human being. Some offenses are so gharsh, and so evil the offended party may cease to see therm as a flawed human being.

The Pathway to Forgiveness

FORGIVENESS from God comes first!

FORGIVE yourself if necessary, let yourself off the hook!

FORGIVE often.

FORGIVE the offender whether they ask for it or not.

FORGIVE over time, it may not be immediate.

Describe the opposite of unforgiveness and bitterness from the verses above.

_____

_____

_____

What does love and forgiveness do to relationships?

_____

_____

_____

Have you ever experienced forgiveness when you knew you didn't deserve it?

_____

_____

_____

Why does forgiveness take some time to be offered?

_____

_____

_____

THE POWER OF CHOICE

Whatever you have been through, and whatever may have happened to you, you still have the power to choose the way you will respond to issues in life. Before you choose to "move out or move on," consider several options:

☐ **You can become bitter.** If you choose to remain angry, seeking a way to cope and make sense of your pain, you can become skeptical and cynical about relationships and reject others the same way you once felt rejected. People tend to get bitter or get better.

☐ **You can become rebellious.** Seeking freedom from any control in your life by rebelling against expectations allows you to establish your identity and significance on your own terms. But to stay that way can keep you from ever meeting in the middle.

☐ **You may become sick.** Seeking attention, affection, sympathy, and care, you elicit the concern and support of others by pronouncing your pain and suffering, whether it be genuine or exaggerated. If you do not work through your issues and move on from them, realize that bitterness will make you sick.

☐ **Or . . . You become useful.** If you choose to become better, seeking a sense of purpose, you will become helpful and give to others. Once you realize that, because you have survived so much, you have a great advantage over other people. Your resilience gives you something to give back to others. You can relate to people in their struggles because you have struggled. Rather than react to other people's anger and stress, you help them work through it as you have dealt with your own.

OUR STRATEGIC GOALS

The following are some of the key goals we have for this program. They will help you find success in managing your stress and anger.

☐ **Develop a sense of Awareness.** Learn to identify your triggers, situations, thoughts, and feelings. When something stressful happens, process the event through your history of success in similar situations. A great part of the battle is become sensitive to when you are triggered and dealing with the triggering source.

☐ **Learn Problem-solving skills.** Life often presents us with problems. People become angry when they do not know how to resolve a situation. Problem-solving helps rectify whatever the issue is. Finding better solutions takes skill and practice.

There are many things we cannot control. What parts of your life over which you do you have the power to choose?

_____

_____

_____

What kinds of characteristics would you expect to see from a bitter person?

_____

_____

_____

How can working through your forgiveness issues make you a better, more useful person?

_____

_____

_____

Describe what forgiveness means to you.

_____

_____

_____

You get to choose to either get bitter or to get better. What has your struggle toward forgiveness been like?

_____

_____

_____

- ☐ **Be Calm.** Go from angry to calm by self-regulating. Take charge of your emotions by calming yourself down.

- ☐ **Create Goal-setting activities.** Goals allow you to work toward something positive and feel proud when you accomplish what you have set out to do. It will give you an incentive for adjusting your old behaviors so you can learn how to control your anger.

- ☐ **Stress and Anger Management Goals:**

    __ "No angry outbursts for a week."

    __ "Asking people specifically for what I need."

    __ "Practicing breathing relaxation techniques daily."

    __ other _____

- ☐ **Practice Impulse Control.** One of the pre-established objectives in anger management is for you to slow your impulses down so you can think before you react to something that triggers you. (thoughts, people, and feelings).

- ☐ **Use Better Communication.** Another goal is for you to learn how to use communication skills rather than reacting through verbal and physical anger, (yelling or violence). "Talk it out before you act it out."

- ☐ **Replace your anger with an intervention.** Learn how to use "I" phrases that will help you communicate how you feel about something that triggers you. Example, "I feel upset when..." and "I have a difficult time when..." or "It would help if you could do blank when . . ."

- ☐ **Be Assertive rather than aggressive.** You will need to discover the difference between acting in an assertive way and acting in an aggressive way. Being assertive is a way of getting your needs met but being aggressive pushes people away.

- ☐ **Manage your stress.** Stress can lead to a loss of control with angry behavioral patterns. By learning how to manage your stress, you can also learn to control your anger.

- ☐ **Adulting.** If acting like an adult has been a challenge for you, then you need to begin the practice of <u>behaving</u> in a way characteristic of a responsible adult, especially the <u>accomplishment</u> of <u>mundane</u> but necessary

Describe an unforgiving person, what are their attitudes and how do they look?

_____

_____

_____

_____

_____

_____

OUR PRIMARY STRATEGIC GOAL

To become <u>assertive,</u> that is, for you to know what you need and not be threatened by getting help. Not aggressive, not passive, but communicative of needs and solutions.

Sometimes, it helps to take a step back away from our lives and assess our relationships. It may be time to ask what kind of relationships we are in, how long we believe they will last, and what it will take to make them work.

MOVE OUT OR MOVE ON

When it comes time to have a heartfelt discussion about your relationship there are some key points to remember:

☐ **Set the discussion in a public, safe place.** If you and the person involved can leave and go somewhere calmer, just the act of changing places can help. Plus, if you're in public you will both be compelled to behave better.

☐ **Breathe.** Learn to breathe deeply so you can oxygenate your brain and think more clearly. If you pay attention, you may notice your breathing to be shallow when you are angry.

☐ **Rethink your position.** When you leave the scene (move on or move out) try to rethink your position in the situation. Do your best to try to think as the other person thinks.

☐ **Forgive.** It may seem strange that I've saved the topic of forgiveness for the end of the book. But the truth is the whole program has been leading up to this moment. Before we give up on a relationship and decide to call it quits it is paramount that we give it a try that we may have never done before.

Have you ever hit the send button on an email or text and instantly regretted it? Never to return, no do over, no opportunity to take back what you said. Someone sent me a scathing text once. When I called to find out what was going on, their response was, "Oh, I sent that to you by accident." Sure, but the information they sent must have been what they were really thinking!

Listening and speaking is like that. It's wise to monitor our words and reactions. They say that's why we have two ears and one mouth, right?

What will be different if you start being assertive rather than aggressive in your relationships:

_____
_____
_____

Let's answer this question: "What I really need in my life right now is:

_____
_____
_____
_____
_____

Describe an unforgiving person, what are their attitudes and how do they look?

_____
_____
_____
_____
_____
_____

☐ Evaluate the relationship.

Take a long, careful look at the past, present, and possible future of the relationship. What does it look like 2 to 5 years from now if nothing changes?

- Has there been any growth and healthy change take place in the last 6 months?
- Do you believe this person is capable of change?
- Have you seen them change for the good before?
- Does the "chemistry" of this relationship create mutual encouragement or erosion?

If your answer is a definite **"no"** without hesitation, then you know it is time to move on.

☐ Envision the consequences.

Make a list of the benefits of staying in the relationship, and what will change if you leave. Are any of the benefits worth staying in the current situation?

- Who pays which bills?
- Can I afford to leave this _____ (job, marriage, relationship)?
- Who will care for the children (if there are any)?
- How capable am I of moving on?

☐ Write everything down.

Keep a log of events good, bad, and ugly. Write dates, events, and how you felt about each of them. (you can go back to the emotions wheel).

Date	Event	Emotion
1/10	He/she called me a _____.	Embarrassed.
1/15	He/she threatened to leave because . . .	Controlled, Manipulated.
2/5	Said they'd call the police and lie, Saying I had done _____.	Endangered.

When you think about evaluating your relationships (especially your primary one) what is most important to you?

___ growth in the relationship
___ healthy change
___ emotional chemistry
___ mutual trust
___ common interests
___ other

What benefits are there to staying in the relationship:

_____
_____
_____
_____
_____
_____
_____

What dangers, risks, and consequences are there of staying in the relationship:

_____
_____
_____
_____
_____
_____
_____

How could keeping a log like the one on this page be beneficial to you?

_____
_____
_____

Build a support team. Look around at the other relationships in your life and seek wise counsel from people you trust will be unbiased and have your best interest at heart.

Cheerleaders	Debbie Downers
_____	_____
_____	_____
_____	_____

Speak to the younger you.
Sit down and put an empty chair in front of you. Envision your younger self sitting in that chair. Then, have a simple conversation about other times in your life you've been at a crossroads.

How did you get through it?

Self-Care, Self-Care, Self-Care.
If you're on an airplane flight, the steward stands in the aisle and carefully explains, "In the possible event that you might need oxygen, the mask will drop down. If you are traveling with a child, make sure you take care of yourself first." They say this because we often have the tendency to take care of others, even to our own detriment. Unfortunately, there may not be enough of ourselves left to help anyone else.

Master these concepts to move forward.
- **FORGIVENESS:** Learn to forgive people who offend you.
- **PLAN:** Plan your own strategic goals for anger management.
- **CHOOSE:** Choose to become better, not bitter.
- **BREATHE:** Practice breathing.
- **MOVE:** Move away from the situation or move on.

Who can you trust to encourage you, and cheer you on to a better you?

_____

Who do you think might doubt or discourage you?

_____

What questions would you ask the "younger you?"

_____

What might the "younger you" want to say that he or she has never shared before?

_____

Define several activities you can engage in to take better care of yourself.

_____

_____

_____

Which concept (s) do you believe you have now mastered from this chapter?

_____

_____

_____

_____

CONCLUSION

CONCLUSION

This has been a great journey we have taken together. There have been moments of discovery and learning, but most of all, it has been a coming to terms with our anger triggers and faulty responses. We have taken ownership of our own issues without blaming others for our faults. Learning to work with anger and stress is a process that can help us for the rest of your life!

We began with understanding anger and defining it in a simple, practical way. Then, we worked at dismantling any excuses for harmful anger. We not only worked at understanding the anger and stress process, but also at understanding ourselves, our personalities, and our tendencies to react.

Then, we learned how to use the CALM Method to deal with any angry episode by:

⇒ Connecting the Dots, by stopping to consider "why" we are angry.

⇒ Asking the right questions, about how we can change ourselves in the situation to find a logical solution.

⇒ Listening, to understand the other person's point of view, and

⇒ Moving out or moving on. When the best we can do is simply to leave the scene.

All we have left to do now is put it all into practice! Dr. Paul

---

Which of the following do you believe you have learned to practice best as a result of this program?

__ *"I learned to **'Connect the Dots,'** discovering root causes and triggers to my anger and stress."*

Explain: _____

_____

_____

__ *"I learned to **'Ask the Right Questions'** as to why I become angry."*

Explain: _____

_____

_____

__ *"I learned to **'Listen to my heart and to Others'** for deeper understanding."*

Explain: _____

_____

_____

__ *"I have made the choice to **'Move Out'** of the situation if and when my anger starts feeling out of control."*

Explain: _____

_____

_____

RESOURCES

www.anxietycentre.com

https://www.anxietycentre.com/anxiety-disorders/stress/

Jim Folk. April, 2021

How to Break the Family Cycle of Addiction.

http://www.boundless.org/adulthood/2014/8-steps-to-break-a-cycle-of-family-dysfunction

The Five Why Process: https://buffer.com/resources/5-whys-process/

www.covenantcc.com

Anger Management Control Tips

http://www.helpguide.org/mental/anger_management_control_tips_techniques.htm

Raymond Chip Tafrate and Howard Kassinove. Anger Management for Everyone, 2019. Impact Publishers. An imprint of New Harbinger Publications, Inc. 5674 Shattuck Avenue. Oakland, CA 94609 www.newharbinger.com

When Her Emotional Tank is Empty.
https://ousoescrever.com/2019/07/19/when-her-emotional-tank-is-empty/

https://pixabay.com/images (all images come from this free website).

www.psychologytoday.com

The Wheel of Emotions. www.pinterest.com/ainarivas (accessed 2023)

Made in the USA
Middletown, DE
19 October 2024